Another Saturday night of wild and reckless abandon

by Cathy Guisewite

Andrews and McMeel
A Universal Press Syndicate Company
Kansas City • New York

 For information write Andrews and McMeel, a Universal Press Syndicate Company, 4900 Main Street, Kansas City, Missouri 64112.

ISBN: 0-8362-1201-0

Library of Congress Catalog Card Number: 82-72415

First Printing, September 1982
Twelfth Printing, November 1990

Two Cathys — I suppose we all could use a couple of Cathys in our lives. The Cathy in Cathy Guisewite's strip is really not the Cathy Guisewite I know. I can tell them apart with no trouble at all.

The comic strip "Cathy" points out for us just how much trouble life is for a young working girl. She shrieks in agony, laughs with delight, and works very hard. I don't know if Cathy Guisewite ever shrieks in agony, but I know she laughs easily, and works very hard. It is not really difficult, in spite of what you may have heard, to draw a comic strip every day, but it is very, very difficult to make it better and better, and this is what Cathy Guisewite has been doing. "Cathy" gets better every day.

I like having two Cathys in my life!

—Charles M. Schulz
Creator of "Peanuts"

Other Cathy books from Andrews and McMeel:

Men Should Come with Instruction Booklets
A Mouthful of Breath Mints and No One to Kiss
Wake Me Up When I'm a Size 5
Thin Thighs in Thirty Years
A Hand to Hold, an Opinion to Reject
Why Do the Right Words Always
  Come Out of the Wrong Mouth?
My Granddaughter Has Fleas
$14 in the Bank and a $200 Face in My Purse

YOU'RE TOO GOOD FOR IRVING, CATHY.
YEAH, I KNOW...

I'M TOO GOOD FOR EMERSON, TOO.

HA! I'M ALSO TOO GOOD FOR RICHARD, PHILLIP, TOM, STEVE, GREG, HENRY, BILL, MARK, BRIAN, TIM, JOHN, BOB, FRED, RON AND JOEY!

I HATE SATURDAY NIGHTS.

RIGHT NOW? OH, NO, IRVING.. ..I REALLY DON'T WANT COMPANY THIS EVENING.

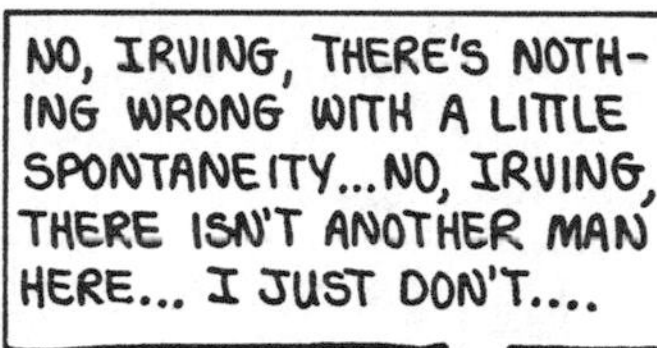
NO, IRVING, THERE'S NOTHING WRONG WITH A LITTLE SPONTANEITY...NO, IRVING, THERE ISN'T ANOTHER MAN HERE... I JUST DON'T....

IRVING, THIS IS NOT A REFLECTION OF MY FEELING TOWARDS OUR RELATIONSHIP ...BELIEVE ME... IRVING, PLEASE...I JUST DON'T WANT COMPANY RIGHT NOW.

ALL IN ALL, IT WOULD HAVE BEEN EASIER TO JUST TELL HIM MY HAIR WAS FILTHY.

THAT'S IT! I'M GOING TO STUFF THE REST OF THESE COOKIES DOWN THE GARBAGE DISPOSAL BEFORE I EAT THEM ALL.

JUST ONE MORE COOKIE, AND THEN THE REST OF THESE ARE GOING DOWN THE GARBAGE DISPOSAL!

OKAY, OKAY, I'LL JUST EAT UP THE BROKEN ONES, BUT THE REST ARE GOING DOWN THAT GARBAGE DISPOSAL!!

GOOD FOR YOU, CATHY. YOU GOT RID OF ALL THE COOKIES.

YOU WANT LOBSTER NEW-BURG, LINGUINI WITH CLAM SAUCE, TURKEY TETRAZZINI...

...CHICKEN PAPRIKASH, LASAGNA, BEEF BURGUNDY CREPES OR SPINACH SOUFFLÉ ?

OH, IRVING, JUST A HAMBURGER WOULD BE FINE.

NAH, THAT'S TOO MUCH WORK.

IS THERE SOME GOOD REASON WHY YOU KEEP POPPING UP AND DOWN OUT OF YOUR CHAIR, CATHY?
YES, ANDREA.
POOL HOURS

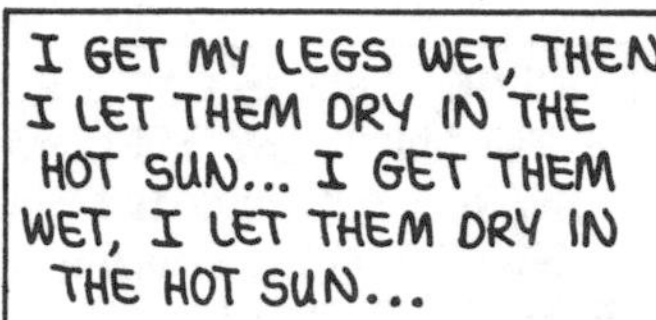
I GET MY LEGS WET, THEN I LET THEM DRY IN THE HOT SUN... I GET THEM WET, I LET THEM DRY IN THE HOT SUN...

POOL HOURS

ISN'T IT A LITTLE LATE IN THE DAY TO BE WORRYING THAT MUCH ABOUT TANNING YOUR LEGS??
I'M NOT TANNING MY LEGS, ANDREA.
POOL HOURS

I'M TRYING TO SEE IF I CAN SHRINK THEM.
POOL HOURS

I'VE BEEN TRYING TO GET A MEETING GOING ALL DAY, CATHY. CAN YOU HELP ME GET EVERYONE IN THE SAME ROOM?
OF COURSE, MR. PINKLEY.

I'M GLAD YOU'VE COME TO RESPECT MY LEADERSHIP ABILITIES, AND I'M PROUD TO DEMONSTRATE THAT SPECIAL, MAGNETIC POWER A BUSINESS WOMAN HAS.

FREE DONUTS!!
PINKLEY

IT'S A LITTLE SOMETHING MY MOTHER TAUGHT ME.

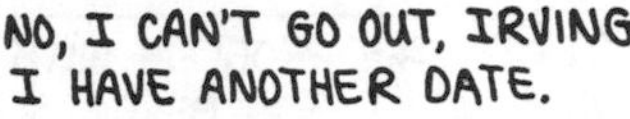
NO, I CAN'T GO OUT, IRVING. I HAVE ANOTHER DATE.

WHY DIDN'T YOU JUST TELL HIM YOU'RE WORKING TO-NIGHT, CATHY ?
I DIDN'T WANT TO GET INTO A BIG DIS-CUSSION ABOUT THE IMPORTANCE OF MY CAREER, ANDREA.

IRVING CAN UNDERSTAND ANOTHER MAN. IT'S A SITU-ATION HE CAN RELATE TO IN A DEEP, PERSONAL WAY.

HE'D RATHER FEEL THREATENED BY SOMETHING HE CAN HIT.
Guisewite

WHAT'S THAT, CATHY ??
THAT WAS A STYRO-FOAM CUP. I SHRED-DED IT TO PIECES WHILE I PLANNED MY STRATEGY FOR THE JACOBS PROJECT.
CATHY

WHAT HAPPENED TO THIS ??
THAT WAS MY CHAIR. I RIPPED OUT ALL THE LOOSE THREADS WHILE I THOUGHT UP MY OUTLINE.
CATHY

I MUTILATED A BOX OF PAPER CLIPS, CHEWED UP 4 PENCILS, AND SCRIBBLED ALL OVER THE PHONE BOOK WHILE I WROTE MY FINAL DRAFT.

I CAN'T CREATE SOME-THING UNLESS I'M DESTROY-ING SOMETHING ELSE.
Guisewite

I WON'T BE IN TODAY, MR. PINKLEY. MY IRON IS THROWING UP.
Guisewite

OH, IRVING, THAT WAS THE MOST BEAUTIFUL MOVIE I'VE EVER SEEN IN MY LIFE!!
OH, CATHY,

QUICK! I HAVE TO TURN OFF THE TV BEFORE THE NEXT COMMERCIAL BREAKS THE MOOD.

QUICK! QUICK!

THAT'S THE PROBLEM WITH YOU, CATHY. YOU NEVER SIT STILL LONG ENOUGH TO APPRECIATE A MOMENT.
Guisewite

"IT IS CRUCIAL FOR THE EXECUTIVE TO LEARN TO DELEGATE RESPONSIBILITY. IF YOU NEED HELP, GET HELP..."

MR. PINKLEY, I NEED HELP. NO HUMAN BEING COULD DO ALL THE WORK I HAVE TO DO.

I'M GLAD YOU STOPPED IN, CATHY. TWENTY-THREE EMPLOYEES HAVE JUST GONE ON SUMMER VACATION, SO YOU'LL HAVE TO COVER FOR THEM.

"...YOU'LL BE AMAZED AT HOW QUICKLY YOUR WORK LOAD WILL CHANGE."
CATHY
Guisewite

OH, IRVING, I'VE BEEN SO BUSY AT WORK.
ME TOO.

I'M JUST EXHAUSTED.
ME TOO.

BUT WE'RE TOGETHER NOW, CATHY. WE CAN JUST RELAX AND ENJOY EACH OTHER.

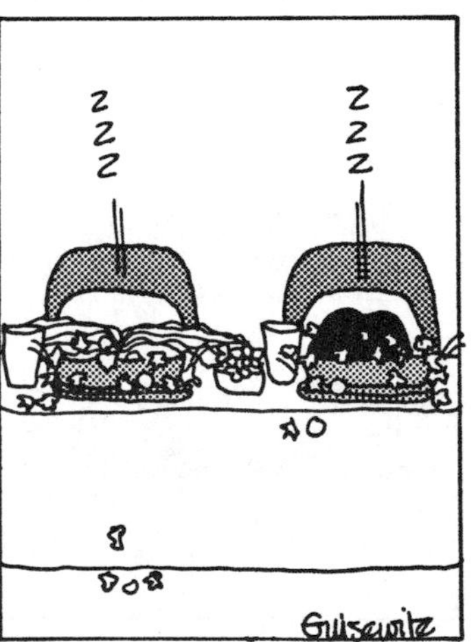
Z Z Z
Z Z Z
Guisewite

MR. PINKLEY, I CANNOT CONTINUE TO DO THE WORK OF 23 PEOPLE WHO ARE ON SUMMER VACATION.

I HAVE TAKEN IT UPON MYSELF TO HIRE A NEW TEMPORARY HELP SERVICE CALLED "M.O.M.".

IT STANDS FOR "MOTHERS ON THE MOVE" AND FRANKLY, MR. PINKLEY, I THINK THE 3 WOMEN THEY'RE SENDING OVER TODAY MAY JUST SAVE...

..MOM!
DON'T SHOUT, SWEETIE. ALL YOUR FILLINGS SHOW.
Guisewite

MOM, WHAT ARE YOU DOING IN MY OFFICE??
WE'RE THE TEMPORARY HELP SERVICE YOU HIRED... "MOTHERS ON THE MOVE".
CATHY

IT'S OUR CONSCIOUSNESS-RAISING PROJECT FOR AUGUST. I TYPE, OLLIE FILES AND FLO BRINGS IN COFFEE CAKE.
CATHY

OH, DON'T WORRY, CATHY. THIS IS STRICTLY BUSINESS. NOBODY WILL EVEN KNOW I'M YOUR MOTHER.
CATHY

YOUNG LADY, YOUR ROOM IS A MESS!!
Guisewite

NO, CATHY ISN'T IN RIGHT NOW. MAY I TAKE A MESSAGE?
YEAH, THIS IS GREGORY.
MOTHERS·ON·THE·MOVE TEMPORARY HELP SERVICE

TELL THAT SWEET THING THAT LAST NIGHT WAS ONLY THE BEGINNING.

WHEN I GET MY ARMS AROUND THAT CUTE LITTLE BODY TONIGHT, WHOOEE! WATCH OUT!!

ANY MESSAGES, MOM?
YES. YOU JUST BROKE UP WITH GREGORY.
MOTHERS·ON·THE·MOVE TEMPORARY HELP SERVICE
Guisewite

ONE
ONE
TWO
TWO
FILE
FILE
MOTHERS-ON-THE-MOVE
TEMPORARY HELP SERVICE

I THINK I'LL GET SOME COFFEE.
ME TOO.
ME TOO.
MOTHERS-ON-THE-MOVE
TEMPORARY HELP SERVICE

I REALLY LIKE HOW YOUR COMPANY MAKES EVERY-THING A TEAM EFFORT, MOM.
OH, YOU HAVE TO STICK TOGETHER WHEN YOU HAVE A SMALL BUSI-NESS LIKE OURS, CATHY.

WE ALWAYS TALK ABOUT WHOEVER ISN'T IN THE ROOM.
Guisewite

WHAT ARE YOU DOING, MOM??
I'M SNOOPING THROUGH YOUR DESK DRAWERS.

WELL! YOU HAD BETTER HAVE A PRETTY GOOD REASON FOR THIS.

OF COURSE I HAVE A GOOD REASON.

I FIGURED THIS WAS WHERE YOU'D HIDE EVERYTHING YOU DIDN'T WANT ME TO FIND IN YOUR APARTMENT.
Guisewite

ONE OF OUR BIGGEST CLIENTS IS COMING IN THIS MORNING, MOM.

WILL YOU RUN OUT AND GET US SOMETHING FOR THE MEETING? YOU KNOW, DONUTS, SWEET ROLLS...
PRODUCT TESTING INC.

GREAT. JUST PUT IT IN THE CONFERENCE ROOM.

HOW ABOUT A NICE BIG BOWL OF OATMEAL, MR. BARCLAY?
Guisewite

$19 ?! HAH! I WOULDN'T PAY $19 FOR A LITTLE LUGGAGE CART.
LUGGAGE CARTS

$35 ?? WHO DO THEY THINK THEY'RE KIDDING ?! I WOULDN'T PAY $35 FOR A LUGGAGE CART.
UGGAGE CARTS
AIRPOR GIFT SHOPP

GATE 64

I'LL GIVE YOU $2000.00 FOR THAT LUGGAGE CART.
ATE 81
GATE 82
Guisewite

WHAT ARE YOU WORKING ON THERE, SWEETHEART ?
I'M SORRY. I CAN'T TALK. I HAVE TO WRITE THIS PRE-SENTATION.

OH ? WHAT KIND OF PRESENTATION IS THAT ?
PLEASE...I HAVE TO GET THIS DONE BEFORE THE PLANE LANDS.

LET ME GUESS...YOU'RE IN SALES, AM I RIGHT ??
FLIGHT ATTENDANT, I HAVE TO CHANGE SEATS. I CAN'T GET ANYTHING DONE HERE.

OH ? WHAT ARE YOU WORKING ON THERE, SWEETHEART ?
Guisewite

HI. THIS IS ROOM 5619. I'D LIKE A WAKE-UP CALL FOR 6:00 A.M. SHARP.
OKAY.

LET ME REPEAT THAT. IT'S NOW 3:00 A.M., AND I WANT A WAKE-UP CALL FOR 6:00 A.M.
FINE. OKAY.

LET ME PUT THAT ANOTHER WAY. I'VE BEEN SLAVING AWAY ON A PRESENTATION AND NOW I WANT YOU TO WAKE ME UP IN 3 HOURS.
IS THERE SOME-THING ELSE, MISS ?

DON'T I GET ANY SYMPATHY ??
Guisewite

NO MATTER WHICH END OF THE AIRPLANE YOU SIT IN, THEY ALWAYS START SERVING FROM THE OTHER END.
AIRLINE GIFTS

SO TODAY, I'M SITTING IN THE MIDDLE. IT'S BETTER TO HAVE A SURE MIDDLE POSITION THAN TO SIT SOMEWHERE ELSE AND BE DISAPPOINTED.
AIRLINE GIFTS
YOU WON'T BE SERVED FIRST IN THE MIDDLE, BUT YOU WILL **NEVER** BE SERVED **LAST**!
SORRY, MA'AM. WE JUST RAN OUT OF FOOD.

CARE FOR A PEANUT ?
Guisewite

YOU COULD HAVE CALLED, CATHY.
IRVING, WE'VE BEEN OVER AND OVER THIS. I DIDN'T HAVE TIME.

YOU COULD HAVE CALLED.
IRVING, I'VE BEEN RUNNING SINCE THE SECOND I LEFT ON THAT BUSINESS TRIP.

JUST ONE LITTLE CALL. HOW LONG DOES IT TAKE TO MAKE ONE LITTLE CALL??

2 HOURS AND 45 MINUTES.
Guisewite

WHAT ARE **YOU** THINKING ABOUT ?
I ASKED **YOU** FIRST, CATHY.
WELL..UM... AHEM.. I WAS THINKING ABOUT OUR FRIENDSHIP, PAUL, AND..UH.. .. I'M..UM... WELL, I'M VERY HAPPY TO BE OUT WITH YOU.

OH... I WAS THINKING ABOUT MY SPEAKERS. DO YOU THINK THEY'D SOUND BETTER OVER HERE ?

I HATE GOING FIRST.
Guisewite

I CAN'T BELIEVE I'M EATING **PIE** AFTER THAT HUGE DINNER PARTY LAST NIGHT!

THAT'S NOTHING. I POLISHED OFF HALF A BOX OF COOKIES BEFORE I **WENT** TO THE DINNER PARTY!

AT LEAST YOU DIDN'T HAVE **BIRTHDAY CAKE** IN THE OFFICE LIKE I DID. HA HA! I JUST CAN'T STOP!

EVERYBODY'S PIGGING OUT, BUT I'M THE ONLY ONE WHO EVER GOES HOME AND GETS FAT.
Guisewite

WHEN I WAS LITTLE I USED TO WATCH MY MOTHER HAVE A CUP OF COFFEE OUT ON THE PORCH ON SATURDAY MORNING.

I ALWAYS THOUGHT, WHAT A WONDERFUL THING... TO BE A WOMAN AND SIT OUT ON THE PORCH ON SATURDAY MORNING DRINKING A CUP OF COFFEE.

WELL, HERE I AM. I'M A WOMAN... I HAVE COFFEE... AND IT'S A BEAUTIFUL SATURDAY MORNING...

NO PORCH.
APARTMENTS
101–401
402–502
Guisewite

IT'S NICE TO SIT BACK ON LABOR DAY AND REFLECT ON YOUR SUMMER ACHIEVEMENTS, ISN'T IT, ANDREA?

YES. LET'S SEE... BESIDES WORKING ALL SUMMER, I READ 36 BOOKS, RAN 5 MILES EVERY DAY...
INVESTMENTS

...ELIMINATED REFINED SUGAR FROM MY DIET, WROTE AND SOLD 4 ESSAYS, AND REDECORATED MY APARTMENT WITH THE EXTRA MONEY I EARNED.

HOW ABOUT YOU, CATHY?
I MADE IT THROUGH ANOTHER YEAR WITHOUT BUYING A TUBE TOP.
Guisewite

I KNOW I USED TO BE JEALOUS AND POSSESSIVE, IRVING, BUT I'M NOT LIKE THAT ANYMORE.
LUNCH

I RESPECT MYSELF, AND I RESPECT YOUR NEED FOR OTHER FRIENDSHIPS.

I'M CALM. I'M RATIONAL. I'M REASONABLE. I AM TOTALLY NON-THREATENED BY WHAT YOU DO OR WHO YOU'RE WITH!

I'VE CHANGED A LOT SINCE 9:30 THIS MORNING.
Guisewite

IRVING'S GOING TO BE FURIOUS THAT I'M NOT READY YET, AND I'M GOING TO GET MAD THAT HE DOESN'T UNDERSTAND MY SCHEDULE.

HE'LL SAY I'M TAKING HIM FOR GRANTED, AND I'LL SAY HE'S BEING PETTY AND UNREASONABLE.

NOTHING WILL GET RESOLVED, WE'LL SULK THROUGH DINNER, AND IT WILL BE ANOTHER TWO WEEKS BEFORE WE GO OUT AGAIN.

WE HAVE A SURE THING GOING.
Guisewite

POTAGE CRESSON À LA CRÈME... SALADE À L'ASPERGE MIMOSA!

GIGOT D'AGNEAU EN CROÛTE.. ..CANARD RÔTI À L'ORANGE... ... ROCHER DE GLACE AUX FRUITES!

MERCI BIEN, MADEMOISELLE ET MONSIEUR. C'ETAIT NOTRE GRAND PLAISIR!

IT RUINS THE WHOLE MEAL WHEN THEY DON'T HAVE A LITTLE BOWL OF MINTS NEXT TO THE DOOR.
HEZ
LIPPE
Guisewite

LOOK HOW SKINNY I WAS IN THIS OLD PICTURE, ANDREA. I THOUGHT I WAS SUCH A TUB THEN.

LOOK AT **THIS**. I THOUGHT I WAS SO FAT WHEN THIS WAS TAKEN... BUT I WAS A LITTLE TWIG.

OLD PICTURES CAN REALLY GIVE YOU A NEW PERSPECTIVE ON YOURSELF, CAN'T THEY, CATHY?
UH HUH...

BRING ON THE HOT FUDGE! I MUST BE THINNER THAN I THINK!

OH, CATHY, LOOK AT THIS...
FALL SALE

CATHY ?...

CATHY ??
Fall Skirts
FALL PANT SALE

HOW MANY TIMES HAVE I TOLD YOU NOT TO GO SHOPPING WHEN YOU'RE HUNGRY?
BLOUSES

EVERY DAY I HAVE LUNCH AT THE SAME PLACE AND EVERY DAY THE SAME MAN IS THERE EATING ALL BY HIMSELF, ANDREA.

YESTERDAY I THOUGHT... MAYBE HE KEEPS GOING THERE BECAUSE HE WANTS TO MEET **ME**... MAYBE HE'S TRYING TO WORK UP THE NERVE TO TALK TO **ME**!

ANDREA, MAYBE THIS MAN JUST LIVES FOR LUNCHTIME SO HE CAN CATCH A GLIMPSE OF **ME**!!

WANT ME TO GO WITH YOU TODAY AND CHECK HIM OUT?
NO... I DON'T WANT TO SCARE HIM OFF.

HI. I'D LIKE TO SEND THAT MAN A DISH OF MACARONI SALAD.
WHAT ?

SEE THAT CUTE MAN OVER THERE ? **TAKE HIM A DISH OF MACARONI SALAD AND PUT IT ON MY BILL** !

WHY ARE YOU LOOKING AT ME LIKE THAT ? HAVEN'T YOU EVER SEEN AN ASSERTIVE WOMAN IN ACTION BEFORE ??!

THAT WOMAN OVER THERE WANTS YOU TO HAVE THIS MACARONI SALAD, SIR.

YES, I AM THE WOMAN WHO SENT THAT MACARONI SALAD OVER TO YOUR TABLE.

I'VE BEEN WATCHING YOU EAT ALL BY YOURSELF HERE FOR THE LAST TWO WEEKS... I FIND YOU IRRESISTIBLE.

I WANTED TO MEET YOU ... AND NOW THAT WE'RE MEETING, **I WANT TO ASK YOU OUT ON A DATE** !!

ALL THINGS CONSIDERED, SHOULDN'T I BE THE ONE WHO JUST PASSED OUT ?

OH, CATHY ! TONIGHT'S THE NIGHT YOU TAKE OUT JOEY, FROM THE RESTAURANT !
THIS IS THE DUMBEST THING I'VE EVER DONE IN MY LIFE, ANDREA.

HOW COULD I ASK A TOTAL STRANGER OUT TO THE MOVIES ?? ALL I KNOW ABOUT HIM IS THAT I LIKE THE WAY HE LOOKS !

THAT **WAS** KIND OF DUMB. YOU WON'T GET TO KNOW SOMEONE AT THE MOVIES.

I WON'T EVEN GET TO **LOOK** AT HIM !!

I SAW JOEY'S APARTMENT TONIGHT, ANDREA...YOU CAN TELL SO MUCH ABOUT A MAN FROM HIS APARTMENT.

IT WAS PERFECT, ANDREA! JOEY IS PERFECT!

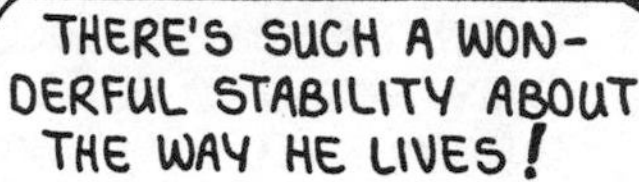
THERE'S SUCH A WONDERFUL STABILITY ABOUT THE WAY HE LIVES!

FINANCE

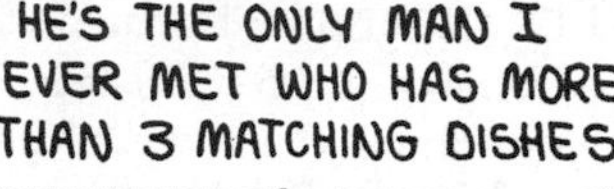
HE'S THE ONLY MAN I EVER MET WHO HAS MORE THAN 3 MATCHING DISHES.

FINANCE
Guisewite

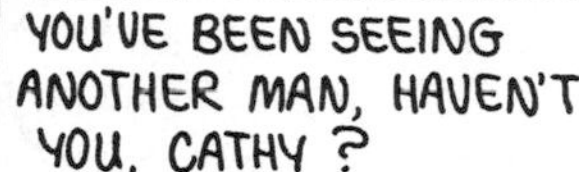
YOU'VE BEEN SEEING ANOTHER MAN, HAVEN'T YOU, CATHY?

DON'T BE RIDICULOUS, IRVING.
RING RING

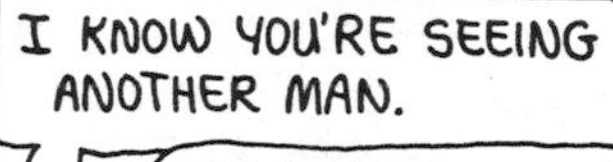
I KNOW YOU'RE SEEING ANOTHER MAN.

IRVING, I AM NOT SEEING ANYONE ELSE.
«RING RING»

OH, HELLO! AHEM, UM.. ...HEE, HEE, HEE, HEE, HEE, HEE, HEE, HEE, HEE, HEE, HEE, HEE, HEE..

THAT WAS MY MOTHER.
Guisewite

OUT? OH, NO...AHEM.. LET'S NOT GO OUT TO DINNER TONIGHT, JOEY.

I'LL JUST COOK SOMETHING HERE.

YES, JOEY! I'LL COOK US A WONDERFUL DINNER RIGHT HERE!

IT WOULD HAVE BEEN EASIER TO JUST GO OUT AND TAKE MY CHANCES ON RUNNING INTO IRVING.
Guisewite

NOBODY PAYS ANY ATTENTION TO THOSE THINGS.

Guisewite

YOU'RE SORRY ?? I LOST 3.4 OUNCES FOR NOTHING!

OF COURSE I'M JEALOUS OF JOEY'S FEELINGS FOR YOU, ANDREA...BUT I CAN HANDLE IT NOW.
YOU CAN?

YES. I STARTED THE RELATIONSHIP WITH JOEY. I WINED HIM. I DINED HIM. I SHOWED HIM THE TOWN.

I'M NOT ABOUT TO GO RUNNING TO MY ROOM TO CRY OVER A LITTLE BOX OF MEMENTOS.

I'M GOING TO GO CRY OVER MY MASTER CHARGE SLIPS.
Guisewite

MY OLD BOYFRIEND IS FURIOUS BECAUSE I HAVE A NEW BOYFRIEND.

MY NEW BOYFRIEND IS IN LOVE WITH MY GIRLFRIEND. MY RENT IS OVERDUE. MY CLOTHES ARE FILTHY, AND I'VE IGNORED MY JOB FOR TWO WEEKS.

THERE'S ONLY ONE THING TO DO...

CRASH!
...GET INTO A CAR WRECK.
Guisewite

WHERE'S THE IDIOT WHO SMASHED INTO MY CAR?!
THAT WOULD BE ME...BUT YOU'RE THE ONE WHO STOPPED WITH NO WARNING.

YEAH, I PROBABLY DID. IT WAS ALL MY FAULT.
WELL, NO..I SHOULD HAVE BEEN WATCHING. IT WAS MY FAULT.

NO, IT WAS MY FAULT!
IT WAS MY FAULT!!

OKAY. IT WAS YOUR FAULT.
THAT'S TWICE NOW YOU'VE STOPPED WITH NO WARNING.
Guisewite

I WAS JUST DRIVING ALONG WHEN SUDDENLY THIS CAR COMES TO A DEAD STOP IN FRONT OF ME...
CATHY

I SLAMMED ON MY BRAKES, BUT THERE JUST WASN'T TIME... I SKIDDED.. ..AND **POW!** RIGHT INTO HER! WELL, YOU CAN....
CATHY

I HAVE A MEETING IN THREE MINUTES, CATHY.
SORRY...I HAVE TO GET THAT REPORT IN.
CATHY

WHAT EVER HAPPENED TO THE GOOD OLD DAYS WHEN A REAR-END COLLISION COULD TAKE UP THE WHOLE MORNING?
CATHY

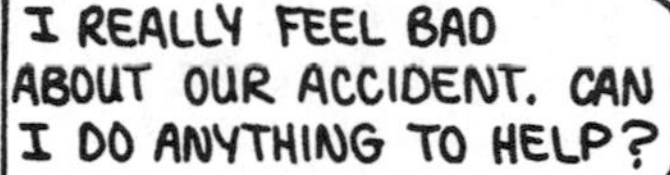
I REALLY FEEL BAD ABOUT OUR ACCIDENT. CAN I DO ANYTHING TO HELP?

NO. THE BOOK I'LL WRITE WILL MORE THAN COVER THE DAMAGES.
JOHNNY
TOWING
SERVICE

BOOK?
YES, BOOK. I WRITE ABOUT EVERY MISERABLE THING THAT HAPPENS TO ME.

I'M A VICTIM OF A MISERABLE WORLD, AND I'M NOT AFRAID TO SAY IT IN PRINT. **I'M MELANIE MORLEY, VICTIM!**

YOU'RE **MELANIE MORLEY?!** YOU HAVE FOUR BEST-SELLERS OUT!!

I KNOW. IT'S BEEN A BAD YEAR.

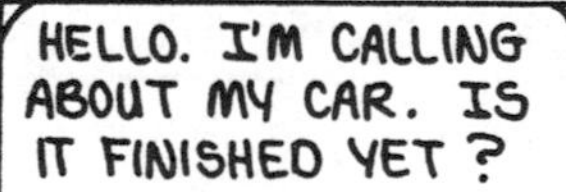
HELLO. I'M CALLING ABOUT MY CAR. IS IT FINISHED YET?

NOT EXACTLY.
CATHY

THE ONLY THING THAT ACTUALLY STILL WORKS ON YOUR CAR IS THE SEAT-BELT BUZZERS.
WHAT?? I CAN'T BELIEVE THIS!

HOW MUCH LONGER IS IT GOING TO TAKE??!
OH, IT SHOULDN'T BE LONG NOW.
CATHY

WE ONLY HAVE ONE MORE THING TO BREAK.
CATHY

I TOLD YOU THAT CAR SERVICE PLACE WOULD RIP YOU OFF, CATHY.
MELANIE, IT ISN'T A RIP-OFF.

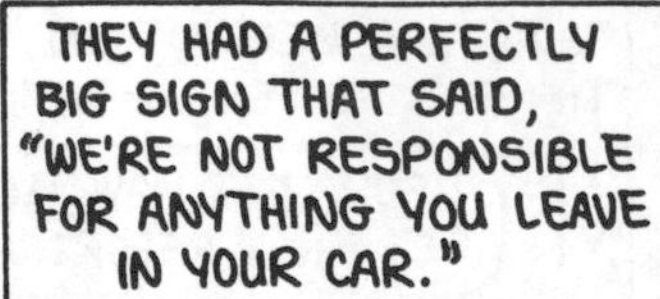
THEY HAD A PERFECTLY BIG SIGN THAT SAID, "WE'RE NOT RESPONSIBLE FOR ANYTHING YOU LEAVE IN YOUR CAR."

I JUST DIDN'T TAKE IT SERIOUSLY.

OH, SWEETIE, WHAT DID YOU LEAVE IN YOUR CAR?
MY ENGINE.
Guisewite

DO YOU REALLY WANT MY OPINION, OR ARE YOU JUST GOING TO IGNORE ME LIKE YOU USUALLY DO?
I WANT YOUR OPINION, MOM.

OKAY. IN MY OPINION, YOU SHOULD GET **MARRIED**. THEN YOU COULD USE YOUR **HUSBAND'S** CAR, AND YOUR TRANSPORTATION PROBLEMS WOULD BE SOLVED!
FINE.

EXCUSE ME, SIR. WOULD YOU LIKE TO GET MARRIED THIS AFTERNOON?
NAH... I DON'T GET OFF UNTIL 10:00.

TOO BAD. HE WAS KIND OF CUTE.
Guisewite

THANKS, MOM. I REALLY NEEDED THIS CUP OF COFFEE.

WANT SOME MORE?
OH NO. I'M WIDE AWAKE NOW.

ONE CUP OF COFFEE AND I'M RARING TO GO!

IT'S DECAFFEINATED.
ZZZZ
Guisewite

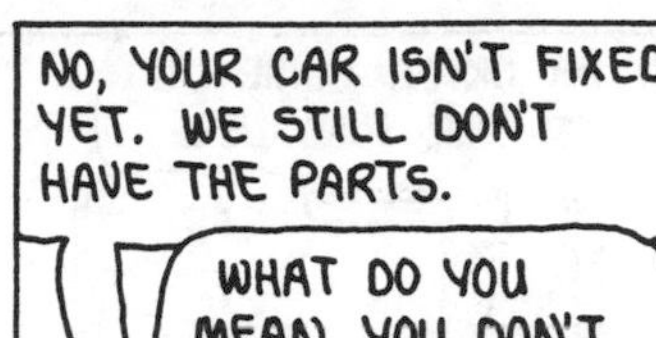

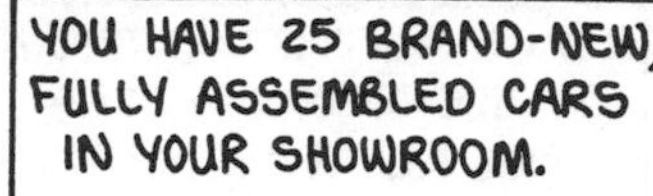

AREN'T YOU GOING TO OFFER ME A DRINK?

Guisewite

I APPRECIATE THE RIDE HOME, MR. PINKLEY... BUT YOU'RE MY **BOSS**.
YOU CAN'T INVITE YOUR BOSS IN FOR A DRINK?

ALL MY OTHER BUSINESS ASSOCIATES HAVE ME IN FOR A DRINK NOW AND THEN.

I'D BE HURT IF YOU THOUGHT SO LITTLE OF OUR PROFES-SIONAL RELATIONSHIP THAT YOU COULDN'T HAVE ME IN FOR A DRINK, CATHY.

OH, OKAY. COME ON IN, MR. PINKLEY.
EARL.
Guisewite

HEH... I'VE NEVER BEEN IN A SINGLE WOMAN'S APARTMENT BEFORE, CATHY.

SO **THIS** IS WHAT IT'S REALLY LIKE! SO **THIS** IS HOW YOU LIVE! SO **THIS** IS WHERE IT ALL HAPPENS!

HA HAH! LET'S DRINK A TOAST TO THE EMANCIPATED WOMAN!

DO YOU WANT DIET PEPSI OR FRESCA?
Guisewite

WHY AM I SO NERVOUS ABOUT HAVING MR. PINKLEY IN FOR A DRINK?

MAYBE IT'S PERFECTLY INNOCENT. MAYBE HE REALLY JUST WANTS A DRINK.

MAYBE HE JUST WANTS TO HAVE A DRINK AND TALK ABOUT BUSINESS.

MAYBE HE ALWAYS TAKES HIS JACKET OFF WHEN HE DRINKS AND TALKS.
Guisewite

MAYBE MR. PINKLEY ALWAYS LOOKS LIKE THAT WHEN HE'S DRINKING...

MAYBE HE JUST MOVED TO THE COUCH BECAUSE THE CHAIR IS UNCOMFORTABLE.. ...MAYBE HIS HAND JUST HAPPENED TO BRUSH MY ARM WHEN HE SAT DOWN...

KISS!

MAYBE HE WAS REACHING FOR A PRETZEL AND HIS MOUTH JUST HIT MY FACE BY ACCIDENT...
Guisewite

MR. PINKLEY, YOU KISSED ME! YOU SAID YOU CAME HERE TO TALK ABOUT BUSINESS!
I DID.

YAHOO! LET'S GET DOWN TO BUSINESS!!

BONK!

SO... WHAT DID YOU THINK OF MY WORK ON THE BAKER PROJECT?
Guisewite

I PUNCHED MY BOSS IN THE NOSE.

MR. PINKLEY! WAKE UP!

WAKE UP! PLEASE WAKE UP!

WHAT AM I GOING TO DO WHEN HE WAKES UP?
Guisewite

WHEN MR. PINKLEY WAKES UP, HE'S GOING TO FIRE ME BECAUSE I PUNCHED HIM IN THE NOSE.

MAYBE HE WON'T FIRE ME. MAYBE HE'LL RESPECT ME FOR REJECTING HIS ADVANCES!

MAYBE I FINALLY KNOCKED SOME SENSE INTO HIM! MAYBE HE'LL REDISCOVER LOVE WITH MRS. PINKLEY AND I'LL BE MADE PRESIDENT OF THE COMPANY!!

MAYBE CHOCOLATE FUDGE BROWNIES DON'T MAKE YOUR FACE BREAK OUT.
Guisewite

WHAT HAPPENED? WHERE AM I??
MR. PINKLEY, YOU'RE AWAKE! I'VE BEEN UP ALL NIGHT WORRYING!

NIGHT?? YIKES! I'M LATE FOR WORK!
MR. PINKLEY, YOU'RE MY BOSS AND YOU SPENT THE NIGHT KNOCKED OUT ON MY FLOOR!
365

SHOULDN'T YOU SAY SOMETHING BESIDES, "I'M LATE FOR WORK"?!
OF COURSE...WHAT WAS I THINKING?
365

YOU'RE LATE FOR WORK.
365
Guisewite

WHISPER WHISPER
WHISPER WHISPER WHISPER

MR. PINKLEY, DID YOU SAY SOMETHING TO THE PEOPLE IN OUR OFFICE?
OH, I MAY HAVE MENTIONED TO CHARLENE THAT I SPENT THE NIGHT AT YOUR PLACE.

CHARLENE?? YOU SAID THAT TO CHARLENE?!! WHY DIDN'T YOU JUST SEND OUT ANNOUNCEMENTS?!!

I THINK CHARLENE IS TAKING CARE OF THAT.
Guisewite

HI CATHY. WHAT'S NEW?
OH ANDREA, I GOT INTO A CAR WRECK...

...MR. PINKLEY GAVE ME A RIDE HOME AND FORCED HIS WAY INTO MY APARTMENT. HE TRIED TO PUT THE MOVES ON ME AND I PUNCHED HIM IN THE NOSE.

NOW HE'S SPREADING TERRIBLE RUMORS AROUND THE OFFICE ABOUT ME... MY REPUTATION IS RUINED.. ..I'M LOSING MY MIND... I..

HI CATHY. WHAT'S NEW?
NOTHING MOM.
Guisewite

CATHY, DO YOU REALIZE THAT SEXUAL HARASSMENT IS POWER PLAY OF THE WORST KIND?
YES!

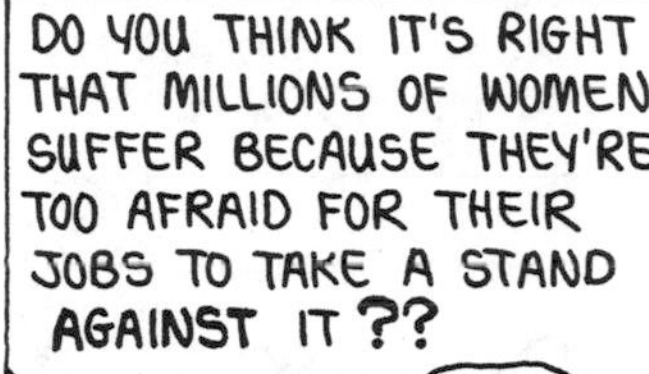
DO YOU THINK IT'S RIGHT THAT MILLIONS OF WOMEN SUFFER BECAUSE THEY'RE TOO AFRAID FOR THEIR JOBS TO TAKE A STAND AGAINST IT??

NO!

ALL RIGHT! THEN WHAT ARE YOU GOING TO DO ABOUT MR. PINKLEY??
I'LL SHOW HIM! I'LL QUIT MY JOB!!

AAAA! WRONG! WRONG! WRONG!
I DO BETTER ON THE "YES" OR "NO" QUESTIONS.
Guisewite

I TOLD CHARLENE EXACTLY WHAT HAPPENED WITH MR. PINKLEY AND SHE SPREAD THE NEWS AROUND THE OFFICE LIKE WILDFIRE.

I DON'T THINK WE'LL EVER HAVE THAT KIND OF PROBLEM AGAIN!

I REALLY LEARNED A LOT FROM ALL OF THIS, ANDREA.
LIFE IS EASIER IF YOU TACKLE YOUR PROBLEMS HEAD ON?

LIFE IS EASIER IF YOU HAVE THE RECEPTIONIST ON YOUR SIDE.
Guisewite

I HAVE TO SLOW DOWN AND START TAKING BETTER CARE OF MYSELF, ANDREA.

I ONLY HAD 1100 CALORIES TODAY.
WHAT'S WRONG WITH THAT ?

YOU'LL PROBABLY FINALLY START LOSING SOME WEIGHT !
FUSSOP CORP.

900 OF THEM WERE FROM NON-DAIRY COFFEE CREAMER.
Guisewite

IT'S BEEN SO LONG SINCE I'VE BEEN ON A DATE I HARDLY KNOW WHAT TO DO.

I'M GOING ON A REGULAR DATE, ANDREA!

A REGULAR DINNER AND THE MOVIES DATE!!

DO YOU THINK I'M OVERDRESSED ?
Guisewite

THIS MILK HAS TODAY'S DATE ON IT. DOES THAT MEAN IT'S ALREADY ROTTEN, OR THAT IT WILL BE ROTTEN TOMORROW ?
I DON'T KNOW.

OR DOES IT MEAN YOU'RE SUPPOSED TO BUY IT BY TODAY, AND THEN IT WON'T GET ROTTEN FOR A WEEK ?
I DON'T KNOW.

WHAT DO YOU MEAN, YOU DON'T KNOW ?
LOOK, I DON'T KNOW. I'LL SEE WHAT I CAN FIND OUT.

ARE YOU CONSULTING YOUR DAIRY BUYER ?
NO. I'M CALLING MY MOTHER.
Guisewite

WHAT HAPPENED, CATHY?
THE WAITRESS DEMANDED THAT I GIVE HER A BIGGER TIP.
Guisewite

I'M SICK OF DRAGGING A PURSE AROUND ALL THE TIME, ANDREA.

WHY SHOULD WOMEN HAVE TO DRAG PURSES AROUND ALL THE TIME?

WOMEN HAVE POCKETS. WOMEN CAN JUST CARRY A FEW NECESSITIES IN OUR POCKETS LIKE MEN DO!

SEE, ANDREA? FREE AT LAST!
Guisewite

WAAH!
HERE, THOMAS. HAVE A COOKIE.

BARB, THAT'S TERRIBLE. WHEN THOMAS IS UNHAPPY, YOU GIVE HIM A COOKIE... WHEN HE'S MAD, YOU GIVE HIM A COOKIE...

THAT IS EXACTLY THE KIND OF TRAINING THAT TURNS PEOPLE INTO ADULTS WHO EAT FOR ALL THE WRONG REASONS!
HERE, CATHY. HAVE A COOKIE.

Guisewite

WHAT TIME DO YOU EAT DINNER, CATHY?
SINGLE PEOPLE DON'T HAVE "DINNER TIME," BARB.

I EAT WHENEVER I CAN FIND A PLATE.

I GUESS YOU KEEP TO A MUCH TIGHTER SCHEDULE NOW THAT YOU'RE MARRIED AND HAVE A BABY.
OF COURSE. WE HAVE TO BE A LOT MORE SYSTEMATIC.

WE HAVE TO FIND THREE PLATES.
Guisewite

TA DA! I'M FINISHED! I CAN'T DO ANYTHING ELSE UNTIL ALL THESE PEOPLE CONTACT ME!!
CATHY

MY PART IS DONE! FINITO! HA, HA! IT'S OUT OF MY HANDS!!
CATHY

KNOCK KNOCK!
RING RING RING!

THAT NEVER LASTS LONG ENOUGH.
Guisewite

SEE IF THE GRAVY HAS ENOUGH SEASONING, CATHY.
THE GRAVY'S GREAT, MOM, BUT THE STUFFING NEEDS A TOUCH OF SOMETHING.

MMM...THE CRANBERRY SAUCE IS PERFECT. HEY, NICE JOB ON THE POTATOES, DAD.
THANKS. THESE VEGETABLES COULD USE A LITTLE BUTTER.

DO YOU THINK THESE ROLLS ARE DONE ENOUGH ?
YEAH, I LIKE THEM THIS WAY. SHOULD THIS SALAD GO IN BOWLS OR PLATES...

OKAY, EVERYONE... THANKSGIVING DINNER IS SERVED!
Guisewite

AACK! CATHY! YOU'RE THROWING ALL THE VITAMINS DOWN THE DRAIN!
WHAT DO YOU WANT ME TO DO, DRINK THE BEAN WATER?!

AACK! IRVING! YOU'RE THROWING ALL THE VITAMINS DOWN THE DRAIN!
WHAT DO YOU WANT ME TO DO, DRINK THE BEAN WATER?!

IT'S GETTING HARDER AND HARDER TO COME AWAY FROM MY MOTHER UNTOUCHED.
Guisewite

I SPENT THE WHOLE MORNING TRYING TO DECIDE IF I'M WORKING HARD OR NOT.

Guisewite

IRVING'S GOING TO RUSH THROUGH THAT DOOR WITH OPEN ARMS, AND HERE I AM, PLANNING AN ARGUMENT.

HE'S GOING TO SAY, "CATHY, MY DARLING!"... AND I'M GOING TO SAY, "IRVING, I'VE HAD IT!"

IRVING ALWAYS GETS ROMANTIC AND SWEET JUST WHEN I'M READY TO FIGHT.

CATHY, I'VE HAD IT!
IRVING, MY DARLING!
Guisewite

SOMETIMES I THINK IRVING TRIES TO BREAK UP WITH ME BEFORE THE HOLIDAYS JUST SO HE WON'T HAVE TO AGONIZE OVER WHAT TO GET ME.
COLOGNE

THAT'S TERRIBLE, CATHY.
COLOGNE

HOW COULD YOU POSSIBLY THINK IRVING WOULD STOOP THAT LOW??
SCARVES

SOMETIMES I THINK ABOUT DOING THE SAME THING.
Guisewite

HI. I'M LOOKING FOR A VERY NICE GIFT. DO YOU HAVE ANYTHING FOR AROUND $40?
OH, YES.

FOR $40 YOU CAN BUY THIS TINY POCKET COMPUTER WITH 37 SEPARATE GENIUS FUNCTIONS OPERATING OFF AN ELECTRIC BRAIN THE SIZE OF A PIN POINT...

OR, FOR $40, YOU CAN BUY THIS WASH'N' WEAR SHIRT.

DO YOU HAVE ANYTHING THAT DOESN'T FORCE ME TO MAKE THAT KIND OF CHOICE?
Guisewite

HOW ABOUT THIS ?
HAH! I WOULDN'T GET THAT FOR IRVING.
CAMERA

HOW ABOUT THIS ?
HAH! I WOULDN'T GET THAT FOR IRVING.

HOW ABOUT THIS ?
HAH! I WOULDN'T GET THAT FOR IRVING.
$AVE SWEATERS

IT'S HARD TO FIND A MEANINGFUL GIFT FOR SOMEONE YOU'RE NOT SPEAKING TO.

HERE...I'LL HELP YOU WITH THESE COOKIES. WHERE'S THE REST OF THE DOUGH?
I ATE IT.

YOU **ATE** IT?? YOU ONLY GOT **NINE** COOKIES OUT OF A RECIPE THAT WAS SUPPOSED TO MAKE 2 DOZEN??

CATHY, I CAN'T BELIEVE THIS!!
NEITHER CAN I.

I USUALLY ONLY GET SIX.

AT FIRST I THOUGHT THIS DRESS WAS TOO SEDUCTIVE, BUT THEN I THOUGHT, "HEY, I'M A 1980'S WOMAN! I CAN BE A LITTLE DARING!"

THE STORES ARE PACKED WITH SLINKY LITTLE NUMBERS FOR THE HOLIDAYS, ANDREA...

...WHY SHOULD **I** BE SELF-CONSCIOUS?!!
OH, SWEETIE, YOU GOT A NEW DRESS! LET ME SEE!

IT'S TOO SEDUCTIVE.
Guisewite

OH MY, HOW THE TIME FLIES!

HERE IT IS, A WEEK BEFORE CHRISTMAS ALREADY!

WHAT ARE YOU DOING ABOUT IRVING'S PRESENT, SWEETIE?

BEGGING MYSELF NOT TO START KNITTING SOMETHING.

ANDREA, I DID IT! I FINALLY FOUND THE PERFECT PRESENT FOR IRVING!!

GREAT...IS YOUR SHOPPING ALL FINISHED NOW, CATHY?
NO. BUT THE REST IS EASY!

WHO DO YOU HAVE LEFT TO BUY PRESENTS FOR?

EVERYONE ELSE.

MRS. BARTLEY! WHAT A SURPRISE.
I JUST WANTED TO DROP OFF A LITTLE GIFT FOR YOU, CATHY.

GIFT?? WELL, WELL! I CERTAINLY WASN'T EXPECTING A GIFT!

HOWEVER...HEH... I DO HAPPEN TO HAVE A LITTLE SOMETHING HERE FOR YOU, TOO.
WHY, THANK YOU, CATHY!

BAD NEWS, ANDREA. I JUST GAVE YOUR CHRISTMAS PRESENT TO MY LANDLADY.

"COLOSSAL HOLIDAY WRAP."
Gift Wrap Center

"... 100 GIANT SQUARE FEET OF GIFT WRAP, 2 FEET WIDE BY 50 FEET LONG!"
OPEN
Gift Wrap

"... YARDS AND YARDS OF BEAUTIFUL DECORATIVE WRAP FOR ALL YOUR GIFT-GIVING OCCASIONS."

Guisewite

I FEEL SICK.

IF I SEE ANOTHER BITE OF FOOD I'M GOING TO BURST.

I THINK MY STOMACH IS EXPLODING.
I HAVE TO LIE DOWN BEFORE MY ZIPPER BREAKS.

I JUST LOVE TO SEE MY FAMILY ENJOY A MEAL!
Guisewite

OH NO. I'M ALL OUT OF ENVELOPES.

JUST WHEN I REALLY GET GOING ON MY THANK YOU NOTES, I ALWAYS RUN OUT OF ENVELOPES.

NOW I HAVE TO STOP EVERYTHING AND GO BUY SOME MORE ENVELOPES.
YOU DIDN'T RUN OUT OF ENVELOPES, CATHY. HERE'S A WHOLE NEW PACKAGE!

Guisewite

CATHY, YOU LOOK WONDERFUL! IS THAT YOUR CHRISTMAS PRESENT FROM IRVING?
SORT OF, MOM.

IRVING GAVE ME THIS BEAUTIFUL SWEATER...

...AND I BOUGHT THIS BLOUSE, SKIRT, SHOES, PURSE, JACKET, SCARF AND BARETTES TO GO WITH IT.

I SPENT $300 MORE ON THE PRESENT HE GAVE ME THAN HE DID.
Guisewite

THIS PLACE IS A MESS.

HOW CAN THIS PLACE BE SUCH A MESS??

I JUST CLEANED UP LAST MONTH!!
Guisewite

WHAT AM I DOING IN BED AT 11:00 ON NEW YEAR'S EVE? THIS IS PATHETIC.

I'M IN THE PRIME OF MY LIFE. IT'S SICKENING THAT I WOULD GO TO BED AT 11:00 ON NEW YEAR'S EVE.

GET UP! DO SOMETHING! DO ANYTHING!! BUT GET OUT OF BED!!

...I SHOULD HAVE STAYED IN BED.
Guisewite

I'M NOT EVEN GOING ON A DIET FOR NEW YEAR'S, ANDREA. I JUST DON'T HAVE THE ENERGY TO START DEPRIVING MYSELF OF THINGS THIS YEAR.

YOU HAVE THE ENERGY TO DO ANYTHING YOU WANT, CATHY.

YOU'RE FULL OF STRENGTH AND DETERMINATION! CATHY, SEARCH WITHIN YOURSELF AND LOOK AT WHAT'S THERE!

17,000 CHRISTMAS COOKIES.

MR. PINKLEY, IT'S FREEZING IN MY OFFICE.
WOMEN ARE ALWAYS FREEZING AT THE OFFICE, CATHY.
PINKLEY

YOU DON'T HEAR THE MEN COMPLAINING, DO YOU?

PINKLEY

YOU DON'T SEE THE MEN BEGGING FOR SPACE HEATERS, DO YOU??
PINKLEY

HA, HA! WHAT MAKES YOU THINK IT SHOULD BE ANY DIFFERENT FOR THE WOMEN?

STUFFED FLOUNDER ON A BED OF RICE!

ARTICHOKE HEARTS ON A BED OF LETTUCE!

CHOCOLATE MOUSSE ON A BED OF MERINGUE!

ME, ON A BED OF CELLULITE.

WHAT DO YOU MEAN, YOU CAN'T FIT INTO ANY OF YOUR CLOTHES, CATHY?
I DON'T KNOW WHAT HAPPENED, ANDREA.

SOMETIME BETWEEN LAST NIGHT AND THIS MORNING, MY ENTIRE BODY GREW ONE SIZE BIGGER THAN EVERYTHING I OWN.

YOU WERE SUPPOSED TO BE ASLEEP!
Guisewite

I'M SURE YOU WANTED TO EAT THOSE COOKIES, BUT THE URGE PASSED, DIDN'T IT, CATHY?

SEE? IF YOU JUST WAIT IT OUT, THE URGE TO EAT COOKIES WILL ALWAYS PASS.

DO YOU KNOW **WHY** THE URGE TO EAT THOSE COOKIES PASSED??

I RAN INTO THE KITCHEN AND ATE 3 DONUTS.
Guisewite

...ONE AND TWO AND ONE AND TWO AND...

...JOG TWO THREE FOUR JOG TWO THREE FOUR...
GASP
GASP
GASP
GASP

GASP! I CAN'T BELIEVE IT! I MADE IT! I GOT INTO THIS DRESS!!
ZIIIIP!!

I'M A LITTLE TIRED TONIGHT, CATHY. LET'S JUST SKIP THE MOVIE.
Guisewite

PERHAPS YOU'D BE INTERESTED IN OPENING ONE OF OUR NEW INTEREST-EARNING CHECKING ACCOUNTS.
ROSE
TAKE ONE

NOW YOUR MONEY CAN ACTUALLY **EARN** MONEY BETWEEN THE TIME OF DE-POSIT AND THE TIME YOU WRITE YOUR CHECKS!

ROSE
TAKE ONE

THE ENTIRE TIME YOUR MONEY IS IN YOUR ACCOUNT IT WILL BE EARNING INTEREST!!
ROSE
TAKE ONE

EXACTLY HOW MUCH INTEREST CAN I EARN IN 17 SECONDS?
ROSE
Guisewitz

APARTMENTS
300-399

VROOM VROOM!

WHY CAN'T YOU GET A DEAD BATTERY LIKE EVERYONE ELSE!!
Guisewitz

JOAN! WAIT!! THESE WERE SUPPOSED TO BE DELIVERED WITH THAT!!

JUST A MINUTE, FRANK! I HAVE TO GET THESE IN TO THE TYPIST!

YES! YES, I HAVE THE PAPERS RIGHT HERE! YES, I'M ON MY WAY, SHARON!

YOU KNOW WHY YOU'RE ALWAYS SO TIRED AFTER WORK, SWEETIE? YOU'RE NOT GETTING ENOUGH EXERCISE.
Guisewitz

VERBAL REINFORCEMENT IS A VERY EFFECTIVE DIETING TOOL, CATHY. AS SOON AS I LEAVE, SAY "I WILL NOT CHEAT ON MY DIET!"

AS SOON AS THIS DOOR CLOSES, SAY IT OUTLOUD, CATHY: "I WILL NOT CHEAT ON MY DIET!"

GO AHEAD, CATHY. SPEAK UP! SAY "I WILL NOT CHEAT ON MY DIET!!"

IT'S HARD TO TALK WHEN MY MOUTH IS FULL.

IRVING, DO YOU REALIZE THAT WHILE WE'RE SITTING HERE WATCHING "FAMILY FEUD" SOMEONE IS WRITING A BRILLIANT NOVEL?

SOMEONE IS PUTTING TOGETHER A MILLION DOLLAR BUSINESS... AND WE'RE EATING A BOWL OF DORITOS.

IRVING, THIS ISN'T ENOUGH FOR ME! I WANT MORE FROM LIFE!!
WE HAVE EACH OTHER, MY DARLING.

RIGHT LINE. WRONG DECADE.

LOOK LIKE AN EXECUTIVE, THINK LIKE AN EXECUTIVE, ACT LIKE AN EXECUTIVE!

LOOK LIKE AN EXECUTIVE, THINK LIKE AN EXECUTIVE, ACT LIKE AN EXECUTIVE!

HEY, CATHY...GOT ANY MORE OF THOSE TWINKIES IN YOUR TOP DRAWER?
NO, I DO NOT HAVE ANY TWINKIES! I AM AN EXECUTIVE!!

IT'S HARD TO CHANGE YOUR REPUTATION IN ONE MORNING.

DO YOU KNOW WHY MEN SUCCEED, CATHY? MEN MAKE PLANS FOR THEIR LIVES.

MEN HAVE 1-YEAR CAREER PLANS, 5-YEAR CAREER PLANS... 10-YEAR CAREER PLANS.

MEN SUCCEED BECAUSE THEY'RE NOT AFRAID TO COMMIT THEMSELVES TO SERIOUS, LONG-RANGE PLANS!

COME ON, SWEETHEART. LIVE FOR THE MOMENT!

I GOT UP AT 7:30 AND RACED TO WORK. I RACED HOME AT 6:30, PICKED UP MY CLEANING, AND SHOVED A FROZEN DINNER IN THE OVEN.

I DID 2 LOADS OF LAUNDRY, RIPPED THROUGH THE PAPER, BEGGED MY LANDLADY TO FIX MY GARBAGE DISPOSAL...

...GLUED A HEEL BACK ON MY SHOE, AND FELL ASLEEP IN FRONT OF THE 11:00 NEWS WITH MY BRIEFCASE ON MY LAP... AND HERE IT IS, MORNING AGAIN.

I CAN'T UNDERSTAND IT, ANDREA. WHY AREN'T I MEETING ANYONE NEW?
OFFICES

IT'S 1:00 AM. I WONDER IF I SHOULD GO HOME NOW. I WONDER IF HE WANTS ME TO GO HOME?
I WONDER IF I WANT TO GO HOME? I WONDER WHAT TIME HIS LAST DATE WENT HOME?

HOW AM I SUPPOSED TO FIGURE OUT WHEN I SHOULD GO HOME??
SURE I CAN'T GET YOU ANYTHING, CATHY?
I'M HAVING A MORAL CRISIS AND HE'S HAVING A BOLOGNA SANDWICH.

WHAT HAPPENED WHILE I WAS IN THE KITCHEN?
THE MAN WITH THE MISTY HAZEL EYES PASSED TO THE GUY WITH THE GORGEOUS LIPS.

THE ONE WITH THE CUTE SEAT STOLE THE BALL AND SHOT IT OVER TO THE GUY WITH THE GLISTENING MUSCLE-Y SHOULDERS.

THEN THE GUY WITH THE FABULOUS JAW TOSSED BACK HIS AUBURN HAIR, AND PASSED TO THE GUY WITH THE GREAT LEGS WHO SMASHED THAT BABY IN FOR A SCORE!!

WHAT ARE YOU SO MAD FOR? I'M STARTING TO LIKE THIS SPORT.
Guisewite

CAN I HELP YOU?
YES. I NEED AN APPOINTMENT CALENDAR THAT WILL HELP ME STAY TOTALLY ORGANIZED.
PENS

HERE... WE HAVE "MONTH-AT-A-GLANCE", "WEEK-AT-A-GLANCE", OR "DAY-AT-A-GLANCE".

HOW MUCH OF YOUR BUSINESS SCHEDULE DID YOU WANT TO SEE AT A TIME?

DO YOU HAVE ANY "MINUTE-AT-A-GLANCE"?
Guisewite

SURE I'LL HELP WITH YOUR RESUME, CATHY... WHAT ARE YOUR MAIN ATTRIBUTES AS A BUSINESSWOMAN?
I'M ARTICULATE, CONSCIENTIOUS, DILIGENT AND ENTHUSIASTIC!

WHAT SPECIAL SKILLS DO YOU HAVE TO OFFER?
I'M ARTICULATE, CONSCIENTIOUS, DILIGENT AND ENTHUSIASTIC!

WHAT HAVE YOU ACHIEVED IN BUSINESS THUS FAR?
I'VE CONTINUED TO BE ARTICULATE, CONSCIENTIOUS, DILIGENT AND ENTHUSIASTIC!

LIFE ISN'T EASY FOR AN ENGLISH MAJOR.

WHY DID I TELL THAT GUY "NO"? I MIGHT HAVE HAD A GREAT TIME.

WHY WON'T I TAKE A CHANCE ON SOMEONE NEW? WHY CAN'T I LEARN TO RELAX AND SAY "YES"??
DING DONG!

HI. DO YOU WANT TO BUY...
YES! YES! YES! YES! YES!

NO DATE TONIGHT, CATHY?
NO. BUT I HAVE 400 NEW MAGAZINE SUBSCRIPTIONS.
Guisewite

I KNOW WHY WOMEN AREN'T PREPARED FOR LIFE, ANDREA. WE WASTED OUR GRADE SCHOOL EDUCATIONS WORRYING ABOUT OUR HAIR.

WE WASTED OUR HIGH-SCHOOL EDUCATIONS WORRYING ABOUT OUR HAIR!

WE WASTED OUR COLLEGE EDUCATIONS WORRYING ABOUT OUR HAIR!!

...ALL THINGS CONSIDERED, SHOULDN'T OUR HAIR LOOK BETTER THAN THIS?
Guisewite

WHEN I WAS YOUNG AND FRUSTRATED, I USED TO GO BUY A NEW RECORD.
WALLER ST.

WHEN I WAS OLDER AND FRUSTRATED, I USED TO GO BUY A NEW OUTFIT.
SALE

NOW I'M EVEN OLDER AND FRUSTRATED... AND SUDDENLY ALL I CAN THINK ABOUT IS BUYING A NEW COUCH.
FINE FURNITURE

THE OLDER I GET, THE MORE IT TAKES TO BUY ME OFF.
Guisewite

YES, MY CONSCIOUSNESS-RAISING GROUP HAS DECIDED TO RAISE MONEY FOR THE EQUAL RIGHTS AMENDMENT, CATHY, AND WE NEED YOUR HELP.

WE WANT OUR GRANDDAUGHTERS TO HAVE OPPORTUNITIES WE NEVER HAD!

OF COURSE I'LL HELP, MOM. I'LL DO ANYTHING TO HELP!

I CAN'T BELIEVE YOUR CONSCIOUSNESS-RAISING GROUP FORMED A **DATING SERVICE** TO RAISE MONEY FOR THE E.R.A., MOM.

IT WASN'T THAT HARD. THERE WERE ONLY SIX OF THEM.

MOTHERS

I DON'T CARE IF JEFF **IS** A 5'10" ACCOUNTANT WITH A BRILLIANT FUTURE WHO LOVES SAILING AND MAKING OMELETTES, MOM. I AM NOT GOING TO CALL HIM UP!

"GORGEOUS BRUNETTE SEEKS TIDY GENTLEMAN WITH WHOLESOME VALUES AND NO BAD HABITS"....BLEAH!

ARE THERE OTHER KIDS IN YOUR FAMILY, JEFF?
I TOLD YOU ALL ABOUT MY FAMILY LAST NIGHT, CATHY.

OH, HEH... OF COURSE. HOW DID YOU LIKE GROWING UP IN PHILADELPHIA?
I'M FROM SAGINAW, REMEMBER? WE TALKED ABOUT SAGINAW FOR AN HOUR.

AHEM... HOW'S THAT STEAK SANDWICH, JEFF??
FINE, THANKS.

I HATE SECOND DATES.
Guisewite

ARE YOU SEEING JEFF AGAIN TONIGHT, CATHY?

I SORT OF EXPECTED I WOULD, ANDREA, BUT I DON'T KNOW...

RELATIONSHIPS BETWEEN MEN AND WOMEN ARE SO CONFUSING NOW I DON'T KNOW WHAT'S GOING ON.

HOW AM I SUPPOSED TO KNOW IF HE'S NOT CALLING ME OR I'M NOT CALLING HIM?
Guisewite

MMM... THIS IS GREAT, CATHY.
"I'M HAVING A WONDERFUL TIME, CATHY. I WISH THIS NIGHT COULD LAST FOREVER."

YOU MADE A PERFECT CHOICE ON THE ICE CREAM!
"YOU'RE BEAUTIFUL, CATHY. YOU FASCINATE ME. YOU'RE THAT EXTRAORDINARY WOMAN I'VE BEEN SEARCHING FOR!!"

UH, YOU'RE NOT TALKING VERY MUCH, CATHY.
I KNOW, JEFF.

IT'S TAKING ME FULL TIME TO MISINTERPRET WHAT YOU'RE SAYING.
Guisewite

HE LOVES ME,
HE LOVES ME NOT.

HE LOVES ME, HE LOVES ME NOT. HE LOVES ME, HE LOVES ME NOT.

HE LOVES ME, HE LOVES ME NOT. LOVES ME, LOVES ME NOT. LOVES ME, LOVES ME NOT. LOVES ME, LOVES ME NOT. LOVES ME, LOVES ME NOT....

GUESS WHAT? YOU LOVE ME.
Guisewite

WHAT ARE YOU THINKING ABOUT, CATHY?
OH, I WAS JUST WATCHING YOU.

I LOVE THE WAY YOUR SOFT GRAY EYES REFLECT EVERYTHING THAT'S GOING ON INSIDE OF YOU.

YEAH, I KNOW... PEOPLE TELL ME THAT ALL THE TIME.
YOU'RE KIDDING.

IT TOOK ME THREE HOURS TO COME UP WITH THAT ONE.
Guisewite

I CAN'T BELIEVE IT! I LOCKED MYSELF OUT!!
SO?... JUST GET A KEY FROM THE MANAGER, CATHY.

JEFF, IT'S 4:00 IN THE MORNING. WHAT'S SHE GOING TO THINK OF ME??

THIS IS HUMILIATING FOR ME, JEFF! IT'S GOING TO RUIN MY REPUTATION IN THE ENTIRE APARTMENT COMPLEX!
MANAGER

OH NO. NOT **YOU** AGAIN.
Guisewite

IRVING!
BEVERLY!
CATHY!
JEFF!

BEVERLY?
IRVING?
JEFF?
CATHY??

JEFF!
BEVERLY!
BEVERLY!
IRVING?

EVERYBODY ALWAYS IGNORES THE WOMAN WHO DOESN'T GET HYSTERICAL.
Guisewite

IT SAID ON YOUR RESUME THAT YOU WERE LOOKING FOR AN INTELLIGENT WOMAN WITH A GOOD SENSE OF HUMOR.
THAT'S RIGHT, CATHY.

OH, ALAN, THAT ISN'T WHAT YOU WANT. YOU WANT TO MEET A WOMAN WHO WILL MAKE YOUR HEART STOP EVERY TIME SHE WALKS INTO THE ROOM!

YOU WANT ELECTRICITY, ALAN! ELECTRICITY!...MAGIC!..YOU WANT THAT GREAT, GRAND, ONCE-IN-A-LIFETIME PASSION THAT EVERYONE WANTS!!

HOW WAS ALAN?
NO SENSE OF HUMOR.
Guisewite

BUT CATHY, JEFF SEEMED SO SENSITIVE AND INTROSPECTIVE...
ANDREA, ON OUR FIRST DATE WE OPENED UP ABOUT ALL OUR VULNERABILITIES,..
CAFET

ON OUR NEXT DATE WE SHARED OUR FEARS...ON OUR LAST DATE WE DISCUSSED THE WAYS WE'D BEEN DUMPED ON AND ABUSED IN PREVIOUS RELATIONSHIPS.

HOW AM I SUPPOSED TO GET EXCITED ABOUT GOING OUT WITH HIM AGAIN?
SPECIALS
TRAYS

WE ALREADY TOLD EACH OTHER ALL THE GOOD STUFF.
Guisewite

7:45. SO WHAT.

8:15... EH, I DON'T HAVE TO GET UP YET.... 8:30... NO PROBLEM.. I STILL HAVE....

YAAACK! I HAVE A MEETING AT 9:00! TOM DRAPE IS COMING AT 9:45! I HAVE TWO REPORTS DUE BY NOON!

SORRY I'M LATE, MR. PINKLEY. IT TOOK ME AWHILE TO START PANICKING THIS MORNING.
Guisewite

I'M OVERQUALIFIED FOR ALL AVAILABLE MANAGEMENT POSITIONS. I'M OVERQUALIFIED FOR CLERICAL WORK.

I'M OVERQUALIFIED FOR ACCOUNTING AND SALES... ...ANDREA, WHAT AM I SUPPOSED TO **DO**??
OH, JUST GO OUT ON YOUR DATE AND DON'T WORRY ABOUT IT TONIGHT, CATHY.

I'M OVERQUALIFIED FOR MY DATE.
Guisewite

AAAAA! THE SLEEVE OF MY JUMPSUIT FELL IN THE TOILET!!
TOWELS

AAAAA! HOW COULD I BE SO STUPID??!
TOWELS

STUPID, STUPID, STUPID!!
PAT, PAT

WE BECOME WHAT WE SNEER AT.
Guisewite

YAAAA! GRAY HAIR!

I HAVE A GRAY HAIR!!

OH, CATHY, THERE'S NOTHING WRONG WITH THAT. FOR HEAVEN'S SAKE. YOU'RE A YOUNG WOMAN!!

YAAAA! OUR DAUGHTER HAS A GRAY HAIR!
Guisewite

I DIDN'T CALL IRVING ALL WEEKEND, ANDREA.

I'M NOT GOING TO CALL IRVING ALL WEEK.... HA, HA! I MAY NEVER CALL IRVING AGAIN!!

WHAT ARE YOU DOING?
I'M GOING TO CALL IRVING.

I WANT TO MAKE SURE HE'S SUFFERING.
Guisewite

I'M ALIENATING MY DAUGHTER BY TRYING TO DO TOO MUCH FOR HER.
MOTHER'S DATING SERVICE

FIRST I TRIED TO GIVE HER ALL MY DISHES FOR HER APARTMENT... THEN I TRIED TO GIVE HER ALL MY FURNITURE AND FOOD... NOW I'M TRYING TO GIVE HER A HUSBAND.
MOTHER'S DATING SERVICE

CATHY! MY BABY! HOW COULD I DO THIS TO YOU?!
OH, HI MOM. I WAS JUST GOING OUT.

TAKE MY CLOTHING, SWEETHEART. IT'S CHILLY OUT.
Guisewite

STEVE IS PICKING ME UP AT 8:00.
ANOTHER BLIND DATE ?
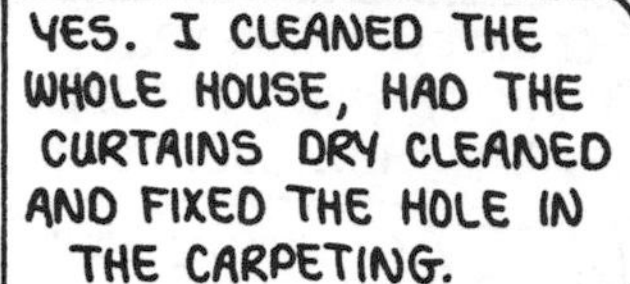
YES. I CLEANED THE WHOLE HOUSE, HAD THE CURTAINS DRY CLEANED AND FIXED THE HOLE IN THE CARPETING.

AFTER DINNER, WE'RE COMING BACK HERE FOR DESSERT. I REFINISHED THE TABLE AND CHAIRS, REORGANIZED THE SHELVES, AND REWIRED THE COFFEE MAKER.

THIS HAS BEEN THE MOST PRODUCTIVE RELATIONSHIP OF MY LIFE AND WE HAVEN'T EVEN MET YET.

CATHY'S GOING TO GO BERSERK, BUT I HAVE TO GET HER EVALUATION OF LAST NIGHT'S DATE.
MOTHER'S DATING SERVICE

THIS IS MY BUSINESS AND IT'S TIME SHE RESPECTED THAT.

APARTMENTS 301-401
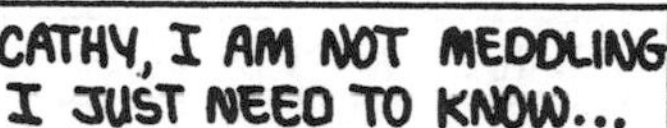
CATHY, I AM NOT MEDDLING I JUST NEED TO KNOW...

MOM, YOU DID IT! STEVE WAS PERFECT! I LOVE YOU! I LOVE YOU!
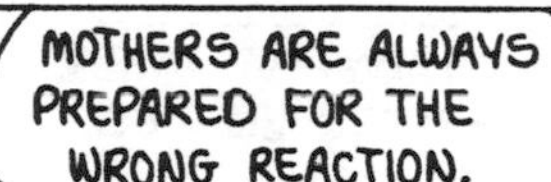
MOTHERS ARE ALWAYS PREPARED FOR THE WRONG REACTION.

...AND THEN BRUCE SAID, "OOPS!" HA, HA...THEN BRUCE TOOK ME TO THE BALLET...BRUCE HAS THE CUTEST CAR...THEN BRUCE...
CATHY

CHARLOTTE, ON BEHALF OF YOUR FAMILY, FRIENDS AND CO-WORKERS, I WOULD LIKE TO SAY WE'RE ALL GETTING A LITTLE BIT SICK OF HEARING ABOUT BRUCE.
CATHY

CAN'T WE HAVE AN INTELLIGENT CONVERSATION BETWEEN TWO WOMEN WITHOUT DRAGGING BRUCE INTO IT EVERY 3 SECONDS?!
CATHY

OKAY, OKAY. WHAT DO YOU WANT TO TALK ABOUT ?
WELL, LAST NIGHT STEVE SAID THE CUTEST THING...
CATHY

"CATHY, YOU LOOK BEAUTIFUL IN THAT DRESS"..."OH, STEVE, HEH, HEH, HEH..."

"CATHY, YOUR COLOGNE IS MAKING ME CRAZY"..."OH STEVE, HEH, HEH, HEH..."

CATHY, WHAT DO YOU THINK OF PHIL'S ANALYSIS OF THE 1982 BUDGET?
OH, STEVE, HEH, HEH, HEH...

I DO TOO HAVE OTHER INTERESTS BESIDES YOU, CATHY.

I HAPPEN TO BE VERY DEVOTED TO YOUR FATHER.

YOU MEAN AFTER ALL THESE YEARS YOU STILL LOVE BEING WITH DAD THAT MUCH?
OF COURSE I DO.

HE'S THE ONLY PERSON I KNOW WHO LIKES TO TALK ABOUT YOU ALL THE TIME.

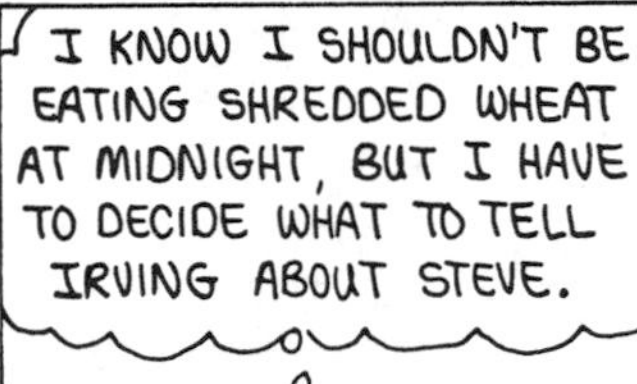
I KNOW I SHOULDN'T BE EATING SHREDDED WHEAT AT MIDNIGHT, BUT I HAVE TO DECIDE WHAT TO TELL IRVING ABOUT STEVE.

I KNOW I SHOULDN'T HAVE A WHOLE BOX OF OATMEAL COOKIES, BUT I HAVE TO FIGURE OUT IF I'M BEING A FREE WOMAN OR A CHEAT.

I KNOW I SHOULDN'T START IN ON THESE BRAN MUFFINS, BUT I HAVE TO GET A GRIP ON WHAT'S RIGHT AND WRONG...I....

MORAL FIBER.

HI. WHICH AISLE IS THE ASPIRIN ON?
OH, IT'S OVER THERE NEXT TO THE OIL PAINTINGS.
WALLER'S DRUG STORE

IT ISN'T OVER HERE.
TRY NEXT TO THE 12-PIECE COOKWARE SETS.
$9.99 OIL PAINTINGS

NO, WAIT... THEY MOVED IT TO THE JUNIOR WEAR SECTION.. NO, WAIT, TRY...
FORGET THE ASPIRIN! DO YOU HAVE ANY DISH SOAP??

DON'T BE RIDICULOUS. THIS IS A DRUG STORE.
Guisewite

YOUR RESUMÉ IS GREAT, JAN. DO YOU HAVE ANY QUESTIONS ABOUT OUR FIRM?
YES, CATHY. I WAS WONDERING WHY YOU HAVE A PICTURE OF MY HUSBAND ON YOUR DESK.

I BEG YOUR PARDON?
THAT'S MY STEVE. YOU HAVE A PICTURE OF MY STEVE ON YOUR DESK.

YAAAAA!!
Guisewite

HELLO, FLO. I WANT TO SPEAK TO MY MOTHER.
ONE MOMENT, PLEASE. WHO SHALL I SAY IS CALLING?
♡MOTHER'S DATING SERVICE

WHAT DO YOU MEAN, WHO'S CALLING? THIS IS CATHY. CATHY, HER DAUGHTER.
THANK YOU. AND WHAT IS THIS IN REGARDS TO?

THIS IS IN REGARDS TO THE MARRIED MAN SHE FIXED ME UP WITH.
OH, I'M SORRY. ANNE IS ON ANOTHER LINE AT THE MOMENT.

YOU DON'T HAVE ANOTHER LINE THERE, FLO!!
SHE'S LISTENING IN ON THE BEDROOM PHONE...
♡MOTHER'S DATING SERVICE
Guisewite

QUIT COVERING FOR MY MOTHER, FLO. YOU KNOW WHERE SHE IS AND I WANT TO SEE HER.
♡ MOTHER'S DATING SERVICE

ANNE CAN'T BE DISTURBED RIGHT NOW. SHE'S IN THE CONFERENCE ROOM.
WHAT CONFERENCE ROOM??
♡ MOTHER'S

THE ONLY ROOM IN THIS HOUSE THAT EVEN HAS A DOOR ON IT IS THE BATHROOM!
HOT PROSPECTS
♡ MOTHER'S
TING SERVICE

GET OUT OF THAT BATHROOM, MOTHER!
ANOTHER HOT ONE HAS SLIPPED PAST THE RECEPTIONIST.
♡ MOTHER'S DATING SERVICE
Guisewite

GET OUT OF THAT BATHROOM, MOM. YOUR DATING SERVICE FIXED ME UP WITH A MARRIED MAN AND I WANT MY 10 BUCKS BACK!
POUND POUND

DON'T SPEAK TO YOUR MOTHER IN THAT TONE OF VOICE, CATHY.

"MOTHER", HAH! YOU'RE THE ONE WHO SAID TO TREAT YOU LIKE I WOULD ANY BUSINESS PERSON!
POUND POUND POUND

DON'T SPEAK TO THE CHAIRMAN OF THE BOARD IN THAT TONE OF VOICE.
Guisewite

STEVE ALWAYS CALLED AT THE STRANGEST TIMES... HE'D ALWAYS GLANCE AROUND TO SEE WHO WAS LOOKING WHEN WE WENT OUT TO LUNCH...
AHAH!

HE ALWAYS WANTED TO JUST LOUNGE AROUND MY PLACE IN THE EVENINGS... AND THE HOME PHONE NUMBER HE GAVE ME WAS A DRY CLEANER'S.
AHAH! AHAH!

HOW WAS I SUPPOSED TO KNOW HE WAS MARRIED, ANDREA?

HE ACTED JUST LIKE MY SINGLE FRIENDS.
Guisewite

I TAKE IT YOUR PHONE CALL TO STEVE DIDN'T GO VERY WELL, CATHY.

NO, AND I DON'T WANT TO TALK TO YOU ABOUT IT, ANDREA.

I AM NOT GOING TO SIT HERE AND WASTE MY TIME PRETENDING LIKE I'M COPING.

I'M GOING TO GO TO THE OFFICE AND PRETEND I'M GETTING SOME WORK DONE.
Guisewite

I KNOW I SPENT A LOT OF TIME WITH HIM, BUT HE WAS NOTHING TO ME...

HE WAS JUST A GUY... YOU'RE WHO I CARE ABOUT. PLEASE... PLEASE GIVE ME ANOTHER CHANCE...

CATHY, I WILL NOT STAND HERE AND LISTEN TO YOU GROVEL TO THAT...
I'M NOT TALKING TO IRVING, ANDREA.

I'M BEGGING MY PLANTS TO COME BACK TO LIFE.
Guisewite

IF I DON'T WASH MY HAIR THIS MORNING, I CAN SLEEP UNTIL 7:45...

IF I DON'T PUT ON ANY MAKE-UP OR IRON MY SKIRT OR DE-LINT MY SWEATER, I CAN SLEEP UNTIL 8:15...

IF I DON'T COMB MY HAIR OR WASH MY FACE OR HAVE ANY COFFEE, I CAN SLEEP UNTIL 8:45...

SORRY I'M LATE. I WAS GETTING MY BEAUTY SLEEP.
PRODUCT TESTING INC.
RECEPTION
Guisewite

HI, CATHY. GEE... I HAD A NOTE TO CALL YOU.
A NOTE?

YOU NEED A NOTE TO REMEMBER TO CALL ME?

IRVING... YOU MEAN I'VE GONE FROM BEING THE LIGHT OF YOUR LIFE TO A NOTE ON YOUR MEMO PAD ??!

CROSS "CALL IRVING" OFF MY LIST OF THINGS TO DO, CHARLENE.
Guisewite

I'VE HAD IT! I'VE HAD IT WITH MEN!!
YOU'RE OVER-REACTING, CATHY.

I'M NOT OVER-REACTING! I'VE WASTED HALF MY LIFE WORRYING ABOUT MEN AND I'M SICK OF IT!!
YOU'RE OVER-REACTING.

FROM NOW ON, I'M SPENDING MY TIME AND ENERGY ON ME, ANDREA. ME!
HOW MANY NIGHT CLASSES DID YOU SIGN UP FOR TODAY?

SEVENTY-TWO.
YOU'RE OVER-REACTING.
Guisewite

MY PLANE FOR DALLAS LEAVES IN AN HOUR, AND I CAN'T GET AWAY, CATHY. WILL YOU MAKE THE TRIP FOR ME?
PINKLEY

CERTAINLY, MR. PINKLEY. I'LL JUST RUN HOME AND PACK A FEW THINGS.
PINKLEY

TICKETING & BAGGAGE CHECK-IN
Guisewite

WHAT ARE YOU GOING TO DO FOR A PRESENTATION, CATHY?
NO PROBLEM, MR. PINKLEY. I'LL WRITE IT ON THE AIRPLANE.
PHONE
GATE 4
FLIGHT
DALLAS

DID YOU HAVE A CHANCE TO GO OVER THE BUDGET?
NO PROBLEM, MR. PINKLEY. I'LL LOOK IT OVER ON THE AIRPLANE.
PHONE

THE MARKET SURVEY...DON'T FORGET THE MARKET SURVEY!
NO PROBLEM, MR. PINKLEY. I'LL FINISH IT ON THE AIRPLANE.

HI. WHAT ARE YOU DOING THERE?
PRAYING WE CIRCLE DALLAS FOR 6 HOURS.
Guisewite

AND THEN JACK SAID...HA, HA! YOU WON'T BELIEVE IT! JACK SAID...
AH, AH, PHIL.. THERE'S A LADY PRESENT.

HEY, C'MON...FORGET IT. LET'S GO ANOTHER ROUND!
BETTER HOLD IT DOWN, SAM. THERE'S A LADY PRESENT.

IF IT MAKES YOU FEEL ANY BETTER, YOU'RE RUINING **MY** LUNCH, TOO.
Guisewite

DID YOU HAND IN YOUR EXPENSE REPORT, CATHY?
CHARLENE, MY MEETINGS LASTED UNTIL 8:00 LAST NIGHT... MY PLANE GOT IN AT MIDNIGHT...
IN
CATHY

I'VE BEEN IN THE OFFICE FOR EXACTLY 25 MINUTES... **WHEN WOULD I HAVE HAD TIME TO DO MY EXPENSE REPORT?!!**

IN
CATHY

OKAY, OKAY. FORGET THE REPORT. WHERE'S THE EXTRA MONEY YOU BROUGHT BACK?
IN
CATHY

I SPENT IT.
IN
CATHY
Guisewite

MY NOSE CAN SMELL SPRING.

MY SHOULDERS AND ARMS CAN FEEL SPRING! MY HANDS AND FEET CAN TOUCH SPRING!!

LOOK OUT, THIGHS. HERE COME THE PASTELS.
Guisewite

I'M STARVING, CATHY. WHEN CAN WE EAT?

WELL, LET'S SEE. ACCORDING TO THIS, DINNER CAN BE READY IN 7 MINUTES.
GREAT.

WHAT CAN I DO TO HELP?

GO BUY ME A CUISINART AND A MICROWAVE OVEN.
Guisewite

WHEN I'M DEPRESSED ABOUT BEING FAT, I STUFF MYSELF WITH JUNK FOOD.

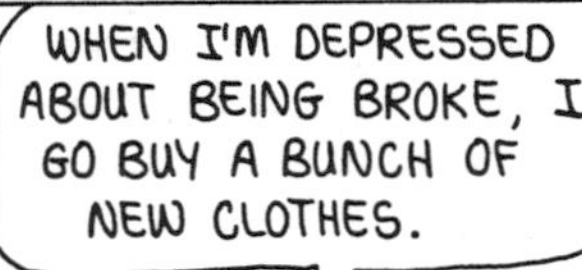
WHEN I'M DEPRESSED ABOUT BEING BROKE, I GO BUY A BUNCH OF NEW CLOTHES.

WHEN I'M DEPRESSED ABOUT A MAN, I JUST SIT HERE IN A STUPOR.

I LIKE IT BETTER WHEN I'M FAT AND BROKE.
Guisewite

PLEASE, CAN'T I JUST GO? I'VE BEEN WAITING FOR 20 MINUTES.
OH, NO. WE NEED THE MANAGER TO "OKAY" YOUR CHECK.

WHY DO WE NEED THE MANAGER'S "OKAY"?? YOU ALREADY TOOK SIX PIECES OF I.D.!
WE STILL NEED THE MANAGER'S "OKAY".

AH, HERE SHE IS.
OKAY.

THANK YOU. HAVE A NICE DAY.
Guisewite

"TAKE A NICE, HOT BUBBLE BATH."... IT'S ALWAYS THE SAME.

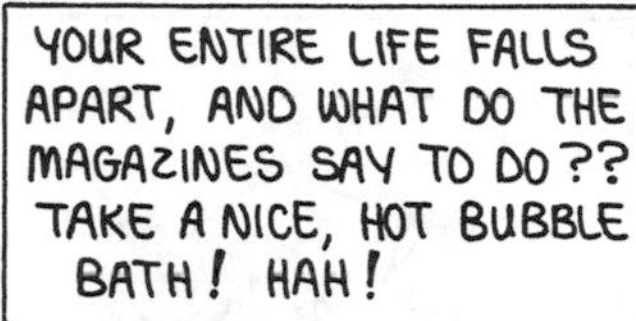
YOUR ENTIRE LIFE FALLS APART, AND WHAT DO THE MAGAZINES SAY TO DO?? TAKE A NICE, HOT BUBBLE BATH! HAH!

I AGREE, CATHY. YOU SHOULD BE USING ALL THAT NEGATIVE ENERGY TO GET YOUR TAX RETURNS DONE, WHICH ARE DUE NEXT WEEK.

NOT NOW, ANDREA. I'M IN THE TUB.
Guisewite

I HATE WORKING ON MY TAXES.

I HATE WORKING ON MY TAXES!

I HATE WORKING ON MY TAXES!!

BAD NEWS, ANDREA. I THINK I JUST ATE MY W-2 FORM.
Guisewite

I MADE $15,000.00 LAST YEAR, AND WHAT DO I HAVE TO SHOW FOR IT?? 45¢!!
WHY ARE YOU ALWAYS SO SHOCKED TO FIND OUT HOW BROKE YOU ARE?

YOU KNOW ABOUT HOW MUCH YOU HAVE IN THE BANK, CATHY.

DID YOU THINK THERE WAS A BUNCH OF MONEY STASHED UNDER THE SEATS OF YOUR CAR OR SOMETHING??

WHERE DO YOU THINK I FOUND THE 45¢?
GUISEWITE

SOFT... SENSUAL... FEMININE... FLIRTATIOUS...

IT'S THE '80 S... IT'S YOU...

...THE NEW ERA OF ROMANCE.
GUISEWITE

WELL, SAY WE WERE BOTH REALLY INVOLVED IN OUR CAREERS...
BEING A PARENT IS A BIG RESPONSIBILITY. WE'D HAVE TO SHARE...

YOU MEAN YOU'D TAKE A LEAVE OF ABSENCE TO RAISE OUR BABY?
WELL, YEAH... I MIGHT TAKE A LEAVE OF ABSENCE...

YOU TWO REALLY SEEM TO BE GETTING ALONG OUT THERE, CATHY.
IT'S THAT NEW INTIMACY, ANDREA.
cowboys
cowgirls

WE'VE ALREADY DECIDED WHO WILL MAKE THE 4:00AM FEEDING, BUT WE DON'T KNOW EACH OTHER'S FIRST NAMES.
TOWELS
GUISEWITE

I HAVE 9 PROJECTS DUE BY FRIDAY, 47 LETTERS TO ANSWER AND 200 PHONE CALLS TO RETURN.

I'M 2 YEARS BEHIND ON MY FILING, I CAN'T FIND MY APPOINTMENT CALENDAR, AND MY SECRETARY'S THREATENING TO QUIT.

AND NOW MY BOYFRIEND, IRVING, WON'T TALK TO ME!
WHY WON'T IRVING TALK TO YOU?

HE'S THREATENED BY MY SUCCESS.

WHY ARE YOU GOING OUT WITH THAT EMERSON TWERP AGAIN, CATHY ??
I LIKE HIM, IRVING. HE'S KIND OF VULNERABLE.

HEY, **I'M** KIND OF VULNERABLE.
HE'S SENSITIVE AND HUMAN, IRVING.

I'M SENSITIVE AND HUMAN!
HE ISN'T RUN BY HIS EGO, IRVING. HE JUST DOESN'T THINK HE'S PERFECT.

I'M LESS PERFECT THAN HE IS!!
WELCOME

THROUGHOUT HISTORY, WOMEN HAVE BEEN SUPPRESSED, REPRESSED AND OPPRESSED, IRVING.

WE'VE HAD MISERABLE JOBS, HIDEOUS PAY, HUMILIATING BENEFITS, AND NOT ONE SHRED OF RESPECT AS EQUAL HUMAN BEINGS.

WHAT POSSIBLE INJUSTICES DO YOU THINK MEN HAVE SUFFERED THAT EVEN COME **CLOSE ???**
WE NEVER LEARNED TO CRY.

YOU NEVER HAD ANYTHING TO CRY ABOUT!!!

I BELIEVE IN EQUALITY. I'M LETTING YOU PAY FOR DINNER, AREN'T I, CATHY?

IRVING, YOU'RE MISSING THE POINT. AS SOON AS YOU SAY "I'M LETTING YOU", YOU IMPLY THAT YOU CONTROL THE SITUATION.

IF YOU THINK EQUALITY IS A MATTER OF PERMISSION, FORGET IT! **YOU** MIGHT AS WELL BE BUYING DINNER!

2 SENTENCES, $31.95.

WHY AREN'T YOU READY FOR WORK YET?
I DON'T HAVE ANYTHING TO WEAR.
345

IT'S TOO WARM FOR MY WINTER CLOTHES, AND TOO COLD FOR MY SUMMER CLOTHES...
I DON'T OWN ONE THING THAT ISN'T STUPID FOR THE END OF APRIL!!
THAT'S RIDICULOUS, CATHY. WHAT DID YOU DO **LAST** YEAR AT THIS TIME?

STOOD HERE SCREAMING THAT I DIDN'T HAVE ANYTHING TO WEAR.

DON'T YOU HAVE A WASTE-BASKET AT THE OFFICE??!

I DIDN'T WANT THE CLEAN-ING PEOPLE TO KNOW I WAS CHEATING ON MY DIET.

Guisewite

ARE YOU FREE FOR A LUNCH MEETING, CATHY?

NO. TODAY IS ALICE'S GOING-AWAY PARTY. HOW ABOUT TOMORROW?

CATHY, QUICK! TOM DRAPE IS ON THE PHONE AGAIN!
I KNOW TOM DRAPE IS ON THE PHONE. I DON'T HAVE HIS PROJECT DONE YET.
SOAP
TOWELS

WELL, YOU HAVE TO SAY **SOMETHING** TO HIM. HE'S CALLED SEVEN TIMES.
WHAT CAN I SAY? THE PROJECT ISN'T DONE!

WHY DON'T YOU JUST TELL HIM THE TRUTH?
I CAN'T, CHARLENE... ...PLEASE, **YOU** TELL HIM THE TRUTH FOR ME.

CATHY CAN'T COME TO THE PHONE, MR. DRAPE. SHE'S HIDING IN THE BATHROOM.
WOMEN
Guisewite

WILL YOU HELP ME SHORTEN THIS SKIRT, MOM?
UP GO THE HEMLINES, DOWN GO THE MORALS.

WHAT?
UP GO THE HEMLINES, DOWN GO THE MORALS!

MOM, REMEMBER WHEN SKIRTS WERE GETTING **LONGER** A FEW YEARS AGO? YOU SAID, "**DOWN** GO THE HEMLINES, DOWN GO THE MORALS!"

HOW DO YOU EXPLAIN THAT??
I'M CHANGING WITH THE TIMES.
Guisewite

IF I TELL IRVING "GOOD-BYE", HE'LL SAY "CATHY, I LOVE YOU". IT'S THE WAY LIFE WORKS, ANDREA.

TELL A MAN "GOODBYE", AND HE'LL SAY "I LOVE YOU" EVERY TIME. "GOODBYE"... "I LOVE YOU"... "GOODBYE"... "I LOVE YOU"...

GOODBYE, IRVING.
SEE 'YA.

HE'S SO UNIQUE.
Guisewite

SINGLE WOMEN ARE REALLY STARTING TO APPRECIATE BEING SINGLE, AND SUDDENLY ALL THE MEN ARE LOOKING FOR COMMITTMENTS.

IT FIGURES. BUT WE'RE NOT GOING TO LET THAT STOP US, CATHY.

WE'VE FOUGHT FOR OUR FREEDOM AND WE'RE GOING TO ENJOY IT!!!

WHO ARE WE GOING TO GO OUT WITH?
Guisewite

I HAVE TO GO TO A MEETING AND CHARLENE QUIT. YOU'RE IN CHARGE OF THE SWITCHBOARD, MR. PINKLEY.

ME? DON'T BE RIDICULOUS, CATHY.

THAT SWITCHBOARD IS A HIGHLY COMPLEX COMPUTER ...AN ELECTRONIC BRAIN CAPABLE OF RECEIVING AND DIRECTING HUNDREDS OF CALLS SIMULTANEOUSLY.

THAT'S WOMAN'S WORK!
RECEPTIONIST
Guisewite

I DON'T THINK I SAW YOUR BEDROOM WHEN YOU GAVE ME THE TOUR...
MY BEDROOM, JOHN?

YES, YOUR BEDROOM, CATHY! WHERE IS THAT BEDROOM??!

NEVER MIND.
Guisewite

I WAS JUST STARTING DINNER, CATHY. WANT TO COME OVER?
OH, NO. I'M TOO BUSY, ANDREA.

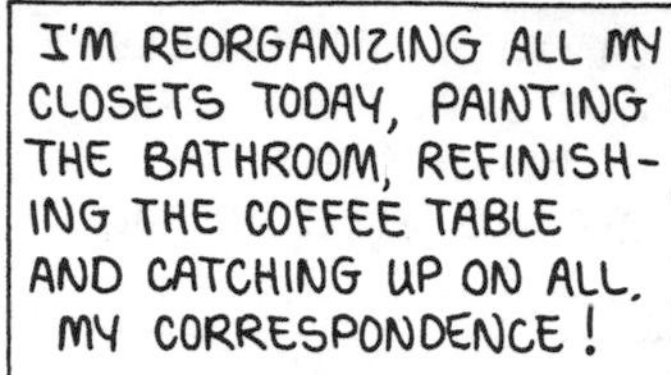
I'M REORGANIZING ALL MY CLOSETS TODAY, PAINTING THE BATHROOM, REFINISHING THE COFFEE TABLE AND CATCHING UP ON ALL MY CORRESPONDENCE!

GOOD FOR YOU, CATHY! HOW'S IT COMING?

IT'S HARD TO SAY. I JUST GOT UP.
Guisewite

PRODUCT TESTING INC... ONE MOMENT PLEASE. PRODUCT TESTING... PLEASE HOLD...
RING RING
RING RING

PROD... HELLO? WAIT A MINUTE... HELLO? YAAACK! WAIT.. PRODUCT JUST A... HELLO HELLO WAIT HOLD ON HELLO...
RING RING
RING RING
RING RING
RING!
RING RING!
RING RING!

YAAAA!
RING RING
RING RING!
CRASH
RING RING

THE SWITCHBOARD BROKE.
Guisewite

GUESS WHAT? ROGER IS MOVING IN WITH JUDY.
THAT'S NICE.
SUGAR
FLOUR

DIANNE AND TOM JUST HAD A BABY AND THEY NAMED IT AFTER DIANNE'S OLD BOYFRIEND.
THAT'S NICE.

CLAUDIA'S GOING ON A 5-DAY CANOE TRIP WITH A GUY SHE MET LAST NIGHT!!
THAT'S NICE.

WHAT'S THE WORLD COMING TO?? I CAN'T SHOCK MY MOTHER ANYMORE.
Guisewite

IT'S FINISHED, MR. PINKLEY!

IT TOOK ME ALL NIGHT, BUT IT'S FINISHED!!

OH, CATHY...HA, HA! GUESS WHAT? WE HAD A MEETING THIS MORNING AND DECIDED TO GO ANOTHER DIRECTION ON THAT.

PINKLEY

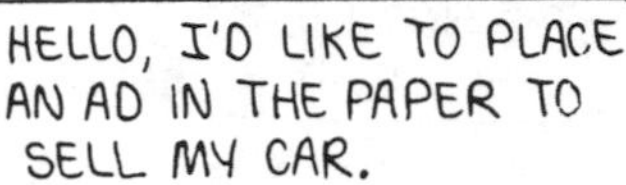

HELLO, I'D LIKE TO PLACE AN AD IN THE PAPER TO SELL MY CAR.
FINE. HOW SHALL IT READ?

"IMMACULATE, PAMPERED, 1975 MODEL WITH STUNNING INTERIOR, MINT BODY, LOVINGLY HAND-WASHED EVERY...."

HA HA HA HA HOO HA HA HA!

YOU DON'T EVEN KNOW ME.

WE KNOW YOU'RE ADVERTISING YOUR CAR IN THE PAPER TODAY, SWEETIE, AND WE'VE COME TO PROTECT YOU.

YOUR FATHER IS AFRAID A BUNCH OF LUNATICS ARE GOING TO COME OVER.

DAD, A BUNCH OF LUNATICS ARE NOT GOING TO COME OVER JUST BECAUSE I HAVE AN AD IN THE PAPER!

WHO ELSE IS GOING TO BUY YOUR CAR?

THEY'RE WELDED TO THE FRUITCAKE IN MY GLOVE COMPARTMENT.

Guisewite

NOT BAD. ZERO TO $950 IN 30 SECONDS.

BROMOL

WHO FORGOT TO TURN OFF THE COFFEE MAKER LAST NIGHT ??
Guisewite

WOMEN GREW UP REPRESSING THEIR HOSTILITIES, AND MEN GREW UP REPRESSING THEIR EMOTIONS.

BUT NOW WE'RE **ALL** LEARNING WE DON'T HAVE TO HOLD THESE THINGS IN ANYMORE.

IT'S REALLY HELPING IRVING AND ME RELATE TO EACH OTHER A WHOLE NEW WAY!
THAT'S WONDERFUL, CATHY.

HE CRIES AND I SCREAM AT HIM.
Guisewite

DO YOU WANT TO GET TOGETHER SOMETIME, CATHY?
NO, TED. ACTUALLY, NO, I DON'T.

WHILE YOU MAY BE ASKING ABOUT THE MOST CASUAL OF DATES, I CAN ONLY SUSPECT YOU HAVE DEEPER INTERESTS, AND IT'S MY RESPONSIBILITY TO TELL YOU I DO NOT SHARE THEM.

EXPERIENCE HAS TAUGHT ME THAT EVEN ONE DATE WITH A MAN I'M NOT ATTRACTED TO IS A MISTAKE. I'M NOT INTERESTED IN ROMANCE WITH YOU, TED. NOT NOW. NOT EVER.

THE ONLY MEN I REALLY COMMUNICATE WITH ARE THE ONES I'LL NEVER SPEAK TO AGAIN.
Guisewite

YOU'RE REALLY AMAZING, CATHY.

YOU'RE AMAZING TOO, IRVING.

YOU JUST ATE $7.00 OF GRAPES IN 16 SECONDS.
Guisewite

"EMPLOYERS OFTEN SURVEY THE OFFICE WASTEBASKETS AFTER HOURS..."

"...AN EMPLOYEE'S PRODUCTIVITY IS USUALLY IN DIRECT PROPORTION TO THE AMOUNT OF TRASH HE OR SHE HAS GENERATED DURING THE DAY."
MANAGEMENT AND YOU

Guisewite

IF A WOMAN'S BORED AND DISGUSTED, DO YOU KNOW WHAT THESE MAGAZINES SAY SHE SHOULD DO?... START HER OWN BUSINESS.

DISILLUSIONED, DEMORALIZED AND DEPRESSED?... "START YOUR OWN BUSINESS!"

FEELING FRAZZLED?... "START YOUR OWN BUSINESS! START YOUR OWN BUSINESS!"

WHAT EVER HAPPENED TO THE GOOD OLD DAYS WHEN WE WERE JUST SUPPOSED TO RUN OUT AND GET A MANICURE?
WOMAN!
Guisewite

HI, CATHY. WANT TO HAVE DINNER?
NO, IRVING. I'M NOT SEEING YOU AGAIN UNTIL YOU CHANGE YOUR WAYS.

...HI, CATHY. I'VE CHANGED.
Guisewite

YOU CAN TELL A LOT ABOUT A WOMAN FROM HER APARTMENT, AND I HAVE TO SAY, I'M VERY IMPRESSED WITH YOURS, CATHY.

IT'S SPOTLESS. IT'S ORGANIZED. THERE'S A REAL ATTENTION TO DETAIL THAT MOST BUSY PEOPLE WOULDN'T TAKE THE TIME FOR.

I SAY WE DRINK A TOAST TO THE WOMAN RESPONSIBLE FOR THIS LOVELY PLACE!
WHY, THANK YOU, JACK.

TO MOTHER.
SOAP

CATHY, IF YOU HATE WHAT YOU'RE DOING, WHY DON'T YOU JUST CHANGE CAREERS?
IT ISN'T THAT EASY, ANDREA.

I MAKE DECISIONS ABOUT MY CARS AND MY APARTMENT... I MAKE DECISIONS ABOUT MY LOVE LIFE...

...BUT MAKING A DECISION ABOUT A NEW CAREER IS A MUCH HARDER THING TO HANDLE.
YEAH, MAYBE YOU'RE...

I CAN'T ASK EVERYONE IN THE OFFICE WHAT I SHOULD DO.

WHAT DO YOU MEAN, YOU DON'T WANT TO GO OUT ANYMORE? WE JUST MET THREE DAYS AGO.

YOU SAID I WAS FASCINATING. I TOLD YOU I WANTED TO KNOW YOU BETTER.

I WASN'T LOOKING FOR SOME BIG COMMITMENT... ..BUT I THOUGHT WE'D GIVE IT A TRY FOR MORE THAN TWO DATES!

GET BACK HERE, JACK! I HAVE 14 NEW OUTFITS TO SHOW YOU!!

WHAT'S THE REASON FOR RETURN ON THESE PANTS?
THEY MAKE ME LOOK LIKE A HIPPOPOTAMUS.
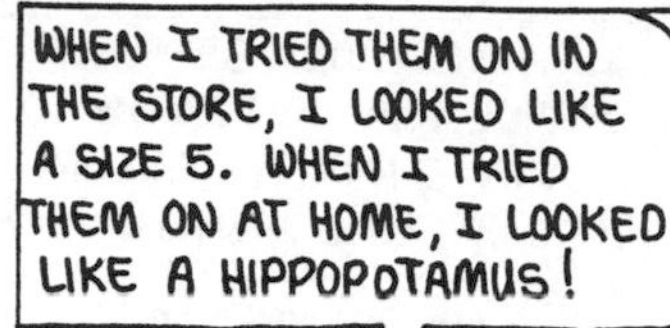
WHEN I TRIED THEM ON IN THE STORE, I LOOKED LIKE A SIZE 5. WHEN I TRIED THEM ON AT HOME, I LOOKED LIKE A HIPPOPOTAMUS!

I THINK YOU PURPOSELY PUT TRICK MIRRORS IN YOUR DRESSING ROOMS AND, FRANKLY, I AM SICK AND TIRED OF IT!
WAIT... TRY THESE. THEY'RE BRAND NEW.

WOW! THESE ARE GREAT! I LOOK LIKE A SIZE 3!!
Guisewite

COME ON, JOE. BE FASCINATING! BE ENDEARING! MAKE ME FEEL HAPPY I WENT ON THIS BLIND DATE WITH YOU.

BE CLEVER, JOE! BE SPONTANEOUS! GIVE ME ENTHUSIASM AND ANECDOTES! CARE ABOUT WHAT I DO!!

COME ON, JOE. YOU CAN DO IT! WIPE THAT GRAVY OFF YOUR CHIN AND BE THE MAN OF MY DREAMS!

I THINK I'M PUTTING TOO MUCH ENERGY INTO THIS RELATIONSHIP.
Guisewite

WHEN I WAS GROWING UP, I ALWAYS THOUGHT I'D END UP NEXT TO MOM WITH A CASSEROLE, NOT NEXT TO YOU WITH A BRIEFCASE, DAD.

BUT HERE WE ARE... AND I WANT YOU TO KNOW HOW MUCH I APPRECIATE THE SPECIAL ENERGY AND DRIVE YOU'VE GIVEN ME FOR BUSINESS.

I AM PROUD TO BE FOLLOWING IN YOUR FOOTSTEPS, DAD!
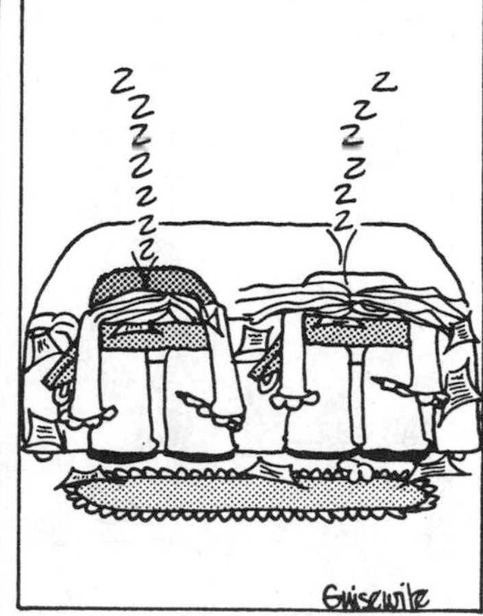
Guisewite

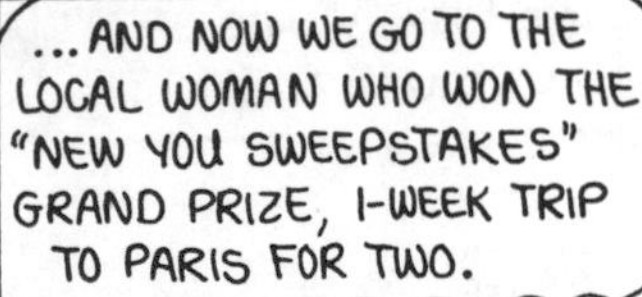
...AND NOW WE GO TO THE LOCAL WOMAN WHO WON THE "NEW YOU SWEEPSTAKES" GRAND PRIZE, 1-WEEK TRIP TO PARIS FOR TWO.

THAT'S MY MOTHER!

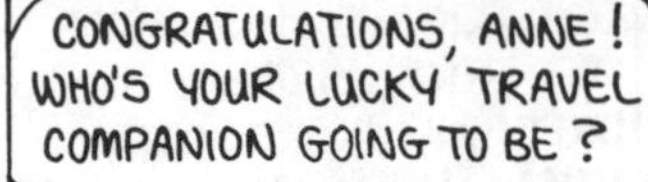
CONGRATULATIONS, ANNE! WHO'S YOUR LUCKY TRAVEL COMPANION GOING TO BE?

I'VE DECIDED TO INVITE MY DAUGHTER, CATHY...

I THINK IT WILL BE A WONDERFUL CHANCE FOR US TO REALLY SHARE THE EXPERIENCE OF BEING A "NEW WOMAN"!
ANY WORDS FOR THAT LUCKY GAL IF SHE'S LISTENING IN?

PUT DOWN THE CORN CHIPS, DEAR. YOU'RE GETTING YOUR FURNITURE ALL GREASY.
Guisewite

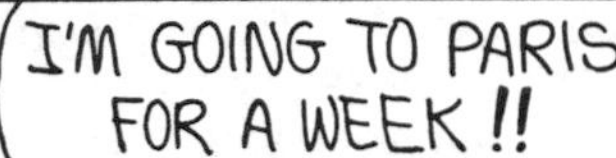
I'M GOING TO PARIS FOR A WEEK!!

PARIS

I'M GOING TO PARIS FOR A WEEK WITH MY MOTHER.
PARIS

I'M GOING TO PARIS FOR A WEEK WITH A WOMAN WHO GETS ON MY NERVES AFTER SIX MINUTES IN THE LIVING ROOM.

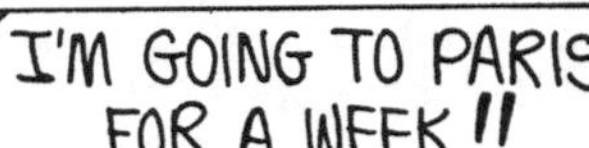
I'M GOING TO PARIS FOR A WEEK!!

Guisewite

I'M ALL PACKED, CATHY.

ALL PACKED FOR WHAT?

I'M ALL PACKED FOR OUR PARISIAN ADVENTURE. AREN'T YOU ALL PACKED?

MOM, OUR PLANE DOESN'T LEAVE FOR **5 DAYS!** OF COURSE I'M NOT PACKED.

I DON'T EVEN KNOW WHAT SIZE I'M GOING TO BE YET.
Guisewite

ARE YOU GOING TO TELL IRVING YOU'RE GOING TO PARIS WITH YOUR MOTHER OR ARE YOU GOING TO INVENT SOME GUY TO MAKE HIM JEALOUS?

ANDREA, IRVING AND I DON'T PLAY THOSE CHILDISH GAMES ANYMORE.

WE HAVE A MATURE RELATIONSHIP FOUNDED ON RESPECT AND MUTUAL APPRECIATION!

WHO ARE YOU GOING TO PARIS WITH, CATHY?
ALAN ALDA.

DO YOU HAVE A PASSPORT?
SURE. REMEMBER PHILLIP? I THOUGHT HE MIGHT INVITE ME TO THE RIVIERA LAST YEAR, SO I GOT A PASSPORT JUST IN CASE.

DO YOU HAVE ANY LIGHT-WEIGHT LUGGAGE?
SURE. REMEMBER JOHN? I HAD A FEEL-ING WE MIGHT RUN OFF INTO THE SUNSET TOGETHER SO I BOUGHT SOME CUTE, MATCH-ING LUGGAGE.

DO YOU HAVE ANY EASY-CARE SUMMER CLOTHES?
SURE. REMEMBER GOOD OLD RICHARD?? I BOUGHT A WHOLE CRUSH-PROOF WARD-ROBE WHEN I WAS DATING HIM.

I HAVE ALL THE RIGHT THINGS FOR ALL THE WRONG REASONS.

YOU'RE LEAVING FOR PARIS **TOMORROW??** CATHY, WHY DIDN'T YOU TELL ME?
I'VE LEARNED FROM THE PAST, IRVING.

RIGHT BEFORE A WOMAN LEAVES FOR A WONDERFUL VACATION, THE MAN SHE LOVES ALWAYS SAYS ONE THING THAT RUINS HER ENTIRE TRIP.

I HAVE SWEET, WONDERFUL MEMORIES OF YOU, IRVING. I DID NOT WANT ONE STUPID PARTING RE-MARK FROM YOU TO HAUNT ME FOR MY WHOLE VACATION.

EH, I COULDN'T HAVE SEEN YOU TONIGHT ANYWAY. I HAVE A DATE.
BINGO.

YOU ALWAYS DO THIS TO ME. YOU KNOW HOW MUCH I HATE RUSHING TO THE AIRPORT AT THE LAST SECOND.

WHAT IF THERE'S AN ACCIDENT ON THE WAY? WHAT IF WE GET A FLAT TIRE?? WOMEN DO NOT THINK AHEAD.

I'M SORRY, BUT IT'S TRUE. IF IT WEREN'T FOR THE MAN IN THE HOUSE, NO ONE WOULD EVER GET TO THE AIRPORT ON TIME!!

HERE YOU GO...YOUR PLANE SHOULD BE READY FOR BOARDING IN 5½ HOURS.
WHEW! WE MADE IT!
Guisewitz

WHAT ARE YOU DOING??
OH, I THOUGHT I'D GET STARTED ON THE HAND WASHABLES.

MOM, WE'VE ONLY BEEN IN PARIS FOR 45 MINUTES! YOU HAVEN'T HAD TIME TO GET ANYTHING DIRTY YET!!

THIS WILL ONLY TAKE A SECOND. DO YOU HAVE ANYTHING YOU WANT TO ADD?

Guisewitz

MOM...STOP...PLEASE! I CAN'T WALK ONE MORE STEP.
STOP?? WE HAVE 9 MORE CATHEDRALS TO SEE THIS MORNING!

I'M BEGGING YOU, MOTHER. LET ME SIT DOWN.
SIT?? HOW CAN YOU SIT??

OKAY, MOM. YOU WIN. I CAN'T KEEP UP. YOU WIN.
DON'T BE SILLY. THIS ISN'T A CONTEST. I'LL JUST JOG UP THE STREET AND BRING YOU A COOL DRINK.

I SEE YOU'RE TRAVELLING WITH YOUR DAUGHTER, TOO.
Guisewitz

I'M SITTING IN A CAFE IN PARIS WITH A WOMAN WHO WOULD LAY DOWN HER LIFE FOR ME. WHY AM I THINKING ABOUT THE MAN WHO FORGOT MY BIRTHDAY LAST YEAR?

I SAW THE EIFFEL TOWER WITH THE WOMAN WHO'S PUT ME FIRST FOR MORE THAN 2 DECADES. WHY WAS I THINKING ABOUT THE MAN WHO DIDN'T CALL FOR 73 DAYS IN A ROW??
TOURS

I TOURED THE LOUVRE WITH THE WOMAN WHO CARES IF I HAVE A HANGNAIL. WHY WAS I THINKING ABOUT THE MAN WHO RAN OFF WITH MY BEST FRIEND WHEN I HAD THE FLU?? WHY? WHY??

WHAT ARE YOU FEELING GUILTY ABOUT? I DIDN'T EVEN SAY ANYTHING YET.
©Guisewite

QUICK! GIVE ME AN ECLAIR! MY MOTHER IS COMING DOWN THE STREET!!
PARDON?
PARIS

DOESN'T **ANYONE** SPEAK ENGLISH HERE?? UNO ECLAIR! PLEASE! MOM WILL BE HERE ANY MINUTE!
PARDON?
PARIS

YOU HAVE EXACTLY FOUR SECONDS TO GIVE ME AN ECLAIR!!
WHAT DO YOU NEED AN ECLAIR FOR? YOU JUST HAD A NICE BIG LUNCH.

SOONER OR LATER, WE ALL REGRET THE DAY WE FLUNKED FRENCH.
PARIS
Guisewite

YOU JUST GAVE THAT CAB DRIVER AN $8.00 TIP FOR A $2.00 RIDE, MOM.
I GOT SO FLUSTERED WITH THE FRANCS I COULDN'T FIGURE IT OUT.
TAXI

MOM, IT IS EVERY WOMAN'S RESPONSIBILITY TO LEARN TO CALCULATE PERCENTAGES AND CURRENCIES RAPIDLY AND ACCURATELY.
FERME
CHEZ

IF WE WANT TO BE TREATED LIKE INTELLIGENT, INDEPENDENT WOMEN, WE HAVE TO **BEHAVE** LIKE INTELLIGENT, INDEPENDENT WOMEN!

HOW MUCH DID YOU TIP THE MAÎTRE D'?
$14.95.
Guisewite

THIS IS STUPID. I'M CHANGING CLOTHES IN THE BATHROOM BECAUSE I DON'T WANT MY MOTHER TO SEE ME IN MY UNDERWEAR.

THE WOMAN GAVE BIRTH TO ME. WHY AM I EMBARRASSED TO HAVE HER SEE ME IN MY UNDERWEAR??

MOM, COME IN HERE A MINUTE. I THINK IT'S...
IF YOU RINSED YOUR THINGS OUT EVERY NIGHT, THEY WOULDN'T GET ALL YELLOW LIKE THAT, SWEETIE.

...I KNEW THERE WAS A REASON.
Guisewite

WHY, THAT WOULD BE VERY NICE! WE'RE UP IN ROOM 1502.

ARE YOU OUT OF YOUR MIND, MOTHER??

YOU HAVE BOUGHT ME $500 OF ANTI-ATTACK DEVICES, AND YOU'RE GIVING YOUR ROOM NUMBER OUT TO A STRANGE MAN IN PARIS?!
OH, FOR HEAVEN'S SAKE, CATHY...

THAT'S THAT NICE MR. BIALKO. HE'S AN AMERICAN.
AH. ONE OF THE GOOD GUYS.
Guisewite

THAT NICE MR. BIALKO INVITED ME TO HAVE CAFÉ AU LAIT WITH HIM. WHAT'S WRONG WITH THAT?
MOM, THAT NICE MR. BIALKO HAS BEEN FOLLOWING YOU AROUND FOR 3 DAYS.

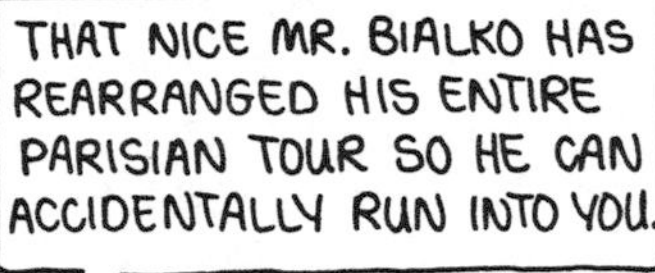
THAT NICE MR. BIALKO HAS REARRANGED HIS ENTIRE PARISIAN TOUR SO HE CAN ACCIDENTALLY RUN INTO YOU.

CAN'T YOU READ BETWEEN THE LINES??
MY GENERATION DOESN'T READ BETWEEN THE LINES, CATHY.

WE CAN NEVER FIND OUR GLASSES.
Guisewite

BONJOUR, MR. BIALKO!
MOM, DON'T ENCOURAGE HIM.
CAFE DE LA PAIX CAFE DE LA PAIX CAFE DE LA P

WHEN A MAN IS INFATUATED WITH YOU, HE WILL MISINTERPRET EVERYTHING YOU SAY.

DE LA PAIX CAFE LA PAIX CAFE

A DESPERATE MAN WILL TAKE EVERY LITTLE WORD, EVERY DECENT GESTURE AS A SIGN OF ENCOURAGEMENT.
FINIS?

OUR WAITER IS IN LOVE WITH ME.
Guisewite

MOM, AM I HALLUCINATING, OR DID YOU JUST PUT ON YOUR BRAND-NEW HAT FOR THAT NICE MR. BIALKO?

AM I DREAMING, OR ARE YOU WEARING YOUR BRAND-NEW HAT BECAUSE YOU'RE A LITTLE BIT FLATTERED BY THAT NICE MR. BIALKO'S ATTENTIONS?

AM I MAKING THIS UP, OR ARE YOU ABOUT TO GO MARCHING AROUND PARIS IN YOUR BRAND-NEW HAT WITH THAT NICE MR. BIALKO WHILE YOUR HUSBAND, MY FATHER, IS ALL ALONE AT HOME WITH A TV DINNER?

AM I IMAGINING THINGS, OR ARE YOU STARTING TO SOUND LIKE YOUR MOTHER?
Guisewite

YAACK! THAT NICE MR. BIALKO THINKS WE'RE HAVING A "LITTLE FLING"!!
I TRIED TO TELL YOU THIS WAS HAPPENING, MOM.

WHAT AM I GOING TO DO, CATHY?? I'LL HAVE TO HIDE IN MY ROOM!
OH NO YOU WON'T.

WE ARE NOT GOING TO WASTE OUR PRECIOUS TIME HIDING FROM A MAN WHO HAS A CRUSH ON YOU. THIS IS OUR VACATION IN **PARIS**!

WE'RE SUPPOSED TO BE WASTING OUR PRECIOUS TIME HIDING FROM A MAN WHO HAS A CRUSH ON **ME**.
Guisewite

SURE I HAVE A MINUTE, ANNE. WHAT'S ON YOUR MIND?
OH, MR. BIALKO, IT SEEMS YOU MIGHT HAVE THE WRONG...

I WHAT?
OH, HEE, HEE, HEE. MY DAUGHTER CATHY THINKS..YOU KNOW...
PARIS

I WHAT?
OH, HEE, HEE, HEE. IT'S SO SILLY. NEVER MIND.

HOW DID I DO, CATHY?
TERRIBLE. YOU HANDLED IT JUST THE WAY I WOULD HAVE.
PARIS
Guisewite

HERE, MOM. LET ME TAKE YOUR PICTURE IN FRONT OF THE ARC DE TRIOMPHE.
OH, I DON'T WANT MY PICTURE TAKEN.

LET ME TAKE ONE OF **YOU**, CATHY.
I DON'T WANT MY PICTURE TAKEN. COME ON... LET ME GET ONE OF YOU.

EXCUSE ME, LADIES. I WOULD BE HAPPY TO TAKE A PICTURE OF THE TWO OF YOU TOGETHER.

IT'S REMARKABLE HOW MUCH YOU LOOK ALIKE.
Guisewite

LOOK, ANDREA, THERE'S IRVING. I HAVEN'T SEEN HIM SINCE I CAME HOME FROM PARIS.
The Hostess will seat you.

HI, IRVING. GUESS WHO?
CATHY. HEY, CATHY, YOU'RE BACK!

I'D KNOW THAT FRAGRANCE ANYWHERE.

MY FABRIC SOFTENER STAYED ON HIS MIND.
The Hostess will seat you.
Guisewite

COME ON IN, CATHY. I WANT YOU TO MEET THE NEW GIRLS I HIRED WHILE YOU WERE ON VACATION.
"WOMEN", MR. PINKLEY, REMEMBER?
PINKLEY

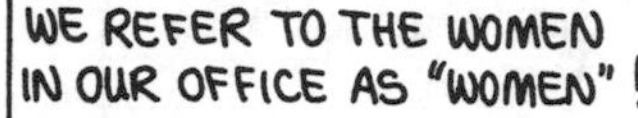
WE REFER TO THE WOMEN IN OUR OFFICE AS "WOMEN"!

HERE'S HEATHER PINKLEY, ROBYN PINKLEY AND CARLA PINKLEY.

I'LL JUST LEAVE YOU WOMEN TO GET ACQUAINTED.

...AND HERE'S JASON PINKLEY, TIMMY PINKLEY, MELISSA PINKLEY, PAUL PINKLEY AND, FINALLY, EARL JR.

MR. PINKLEY, I HAVE BEEN WITH THIS COMPANY FOR 4½ YEARS. I TOOK A ONE-WEEK VACATION, AND YOU HIRED 12 INEXPERIENCED RELATIVES OVER MY HEAD.
PINKLEY

HAVE MY HARD WORK AND DEVOTION EARNED ME A SPECIAL PLACE IN THIS COMPANY OR NOT??
OF COURSE YOU HAVE A SPECIAL PLACE HERE, CATHY.

YOU'RE THE ONLY ONE WHO ISN'T A PINKLEY!!

ARE YOU COMFORTABLE, IRVING?
SURE I'M COMFORTABLE. ARE YOU OKAY?

OF COURSE I'M OKAY. I THOUGHT YOUR LEGS MIGHT BE FALLING ASLEEP.
ASLEEP? HAH! NOT MINE.

YOU KIDDING? I EAT AT JAPANESE RESTAURANTS ALL THE TIME! SUSHI! SAKE! TATAMI! LOVE IT!

WANT ME TO DRIVE?
DON'T BE RIDICULOUS.

THERE'S NO ANSWER. HOW CAN THERE BE NO ANSWER? HE HAS AN ANSWERING MACHINE.
RING RING RING RING

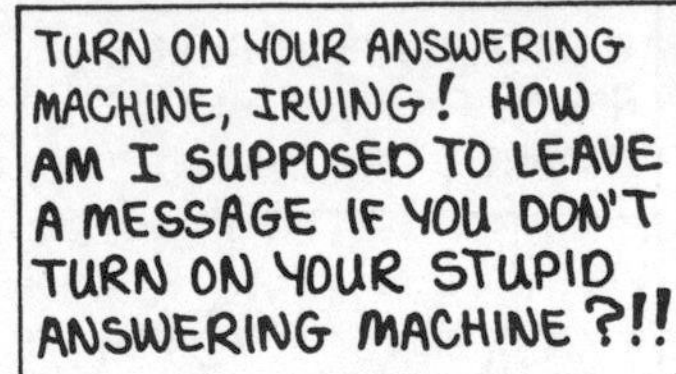
TURN ON YOUR ANSWERING MACHINE, IRVING! HOW AM I SUPPOSED TO LEAVE A MESSAGE IF YOU DON'T TURN ON YOUR STUPID ANSWERING MACHINE?!!

RING RING RING RING

WHAT'S WRONG WITH **YOU**, CATHY?

I'M MAD BECAUSE I DIDN'T GET A RECORDING.

ARE YOU DATING ANYONE, CATHY?
WELL, I'VE BEEN SEEING THIS GUY NAMED IRVING, BUT WE STILL GO OUT WITH OTHER PEOPLE.

I GO OUT WITH A WOMAN NAMED SUSAN, BUT IT ISN'T SERIOUS.

I OCCASIONALLY DATE EMERSON, BUT THERE REALLY ISN'T A FUTURE THERE.

I'VE BEEN SEEING PAULA... ...NAH, PAULA MEANS NOTHING TO ME.
ARE YOU READY TO LEAVE YET, CATHY?

NOT QUITE. DONALD AND I ARE STILL REVIEWING OUR PRIOR LACK-OF-COMMITMENTS.

HI, MOM. HOW WAS YOUR MEETING?
TERRIBLE. THOSE WOMEN HAVE NO SENSE OF PURPOSE.

MY ENTIRE CONSCIOUSNESS-RAISING SESSION DETERIORATED INTO A CHEAP FIGHT OVER WHOSE DAUGHTER SHOULD BE MARRYING PRINCE CHARLES.

OH, MOM... I'M SORRY.

HE NEVER EVEN GOT TO **MEET** YOU!!

NO, MR. PINKLEY. NO, I WILL NOT BE IN THE OFFICE TODAY.

I WILL NOT BE IN THE OFFICE BECAUSE PRINCE CHARLES IS GETTING MARRIED TODAY.

THIS IS VERY IMPORTANT, MR. PINKLEY. FOR WOMEN MY AGE, THIS EVENT HAS A VERY SPECIAL MEANING...

... OUR MOTHERS NEED US.
TISSUE
Guisewite

HELLO, IRVING? OH, IRVING, I'VE BEEN SO PREOCCUPIED... IT'S BEEN SO LONG SINCE I TOLD YOU HOW MUCH I CARE...

I **DO** CARE, IRVING. I LOVE YOU. I ADORE YOU. YOU'RE THE MOST SPECIAL PERSON IN THE WORLD TO ME!!

ASK IF HE HAS COMPANY, FIRST. OPEN BIG MOUTH, SECOND.
Guisewite

THAT SOUNDS LIKE FUN!
GREAT! JUST RUN IN AND THROW ON SOME JEANS AND A T-SHIRT.

DIRTY... DIRTY... TOO TIGHT... DIRTY... TOO SHORT ... TOO TIGHT... DIRTY...

TOO TIGHT... NO BUTTONS... DIRTY... GIANT HOLE... BROKEN ZIPPER... TOO TIGHT... TOO UGLY...

SORRY, HENRY. I'M NOT PREPARED TO BE SPONTANEOUS.
Guisewite

YAACK! TOM DRAPE IS EXPECTING TO SEE THIS PROJECT IN TWO HOURS!
YAACK! I CAN'T FIND THE FILES!

YAACK! I JUST REMEMBERED WE WERE SUPPOSED TO RE-DO ALL THESE CHARTS!
YAACK! THE COPY MACHINE JAMMED UP!

YAACK! SOMEONE ATE LUNCH ON MY 1983 PROJECTION SHEETS!
YAACK! MY ROLADEX JUST DUMPED OUT ALL OVER THE FLOOR!

HI, CATHY. WHAT ARE YOU UP TO?
WE WERE JUST YAKKING.
Guisewite

"CHICKEN FOR 8"..."LASAGNA FOR 6"..."FISH STICKS FOR 12"...SEE WHAT I MEAN, MOM?
FISH STICKS

FOOD COMPANIES DO NOT UNDERSTAND THE NEEDS OF THE SINGLE PERSON.

"PIE FOR 2"...HERE, CATHY. WHAT'S WRONG WITH THIS?

IT DOESN'T HAVE ENOUGH SERVINGS.
Guisewite

THIS MAN WANTS TO KISS ME. HE'S PUT OFF GOING HOME FOR 2 HOURS TRYING TO WORK UP THE NERVE TO KISS ME.

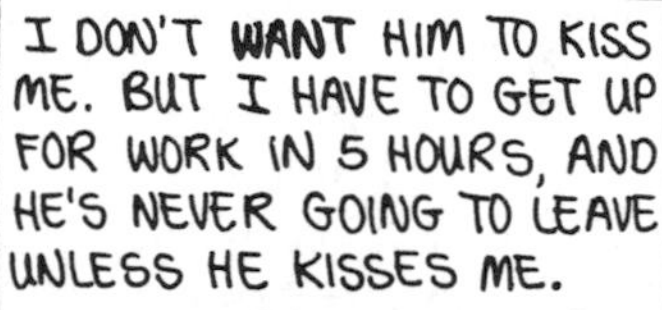
I DON'T **WANT** HIM TO KISS ME. BUT I HAVE TO GET UP FOR WORK IN 5 HOURS, AND HE'S NEVER GOING TO LEAVE UNLESS HE KISSES ME.

WILL YOU JUST KISS ME AND GET IT OVER WITH??

HOW DID IT GO WITH JACK LAST NIGHT?
HE SAID I WAS TOO PUSHY.
Guisewite

YOU DO TOO HAVE FOOD IN YOUR REFRIGERATOR, CATHY. LOOK AT ALL THIS CHEESE.
THAT'S THE WORST CHEESE I EVER TASTED IN MY LIFE, ANDREA.

IT LOOKED GOOD IN THE STORE, BUT IT'S DISGUSTING. I CAN'T EAT IT.

IF IT'S THAT DISGUSTING, WHAT'S IT DOING IN YOUR REFRIGERATOR?

I WAS SAVING IT FOR COMPANY.

$7.25?! HOW COULD YOU PAY $7.25 FOR A 1-POUND CAN OF COFFEE?!
COFFEE

I WAS IN A HURRY, MOM. I STOPPED AT THE LITTLE CONVENIENCE STORE.
OH, CATHY...

...DON'T YOU REMEMBER THE ONE SIMPLE RULE WE HAVE ABOUT GROCERY SHOPPING??
YES, MOM.

ALWAYS RIP OFF THE PRICE STICKERS BEFORE MOTHER COMES TO VISIT.

I CAN MAKE A GREAT OMELETTE, CATHY. WHERE'S YOUR FRYING PAN?
MY FRYING PAN?... ...AHEM...JUST A MINUTE, PAUL.

JUST SHUT YOUR EYES AND I WILL BRING YOU MY FRYING PAN!

SCOUR
SCRUB
SCOUR
SCRUB
SCRUB
SCOUR
SCOUR

YOU'RE PEEKING.
SCOUR

RING
RING
RING

Guisewite

DID YOU LET IRVING HAVE IT FOR NOT SHOWING UP LAST NIGHT, CATHY?
I WAS FURIOUS LAST NIGHT, ANDREA.

BUT THEN I STARTED THINKING... WAS WHAT HE DID ACTUALLY ANY WORSE THAN SOME OF THE THINGS I'VE DONE?

I'VE BEEN THOUGHTLESS AND INCONSIDERATE... I'VE GOTTEN MYSELF INTO MESSES... I'VE HURT SOME FINE PEOPLE, ANDREA.. I'VE DONE HORRIBLE THINGS!!

WHAT DID YOU SAY TO IRVING?
SOMEHOW I WOUND UP BEGGING HIM TO FORGIVE ME.
Guisewite

I DON'T SEEM TO HAVE ANY MONEY IN HERE. WILL YOU TAKE A CHECK?

OH, I DON'T SEEM TO HAVE A PEN. MAY I BORROW... ...NEVER MIND.. I DON'T SEEM TO HAVE MY CHECK-BOOK WITH ME.

WILL YOU TAKE A CHARGE CARD? AHEM... WAIT... I DON'T SEEM TO HAVE MY CHARGE CARDS WITH ME, EITHER.

HOW EMBARRASSING. I'VE BEEN CARRYING AROUND 300 GUM WRAPPERS FOR THE LAST FOUR DAYS.
Guisewite

MEN INVEST THEIR MONEY IN THE STOCK MARKET AND WOMEN SPEND THEIR MONEY ON MAKE-UP SO WE CAN LURE THEM.

NOTHING'S CHANGED, ANDREA. IRVING'S OUT THERE BUILDING A FINANCIAL FUTURE FOR HIMSELF AND WHAT DO I HAVE? "GLIMMERY ROSE-BUD" CHEEKS!

CATHY, THERE IS **ONE** REASON AND **ONE REASON** ALONE WHY A MAN LIKE IRVING IS INVESTING HIS MONEY MORE PRODUCTIVELY THAN YOU!

HE HAS $5000.00 AND I HAVE 89¢.
Guisewite

"DEAR MIDLAND HIGH SCHOOL GRADUATE, PLEASE JOIN US AT OUR CLASS REUNION, AUGUST 28, 1981."

"THIS IS YOUR CHANCE TO HAVE 600 EX-CLASSMATES STARE AT YOU AND SEE WHETHER YOU GOT FAT AND/OR WOUND UP WITH A LOSER!.."

"IN ONE FUN-FILLED EVENING, WE WILL RE-CREATE EVERY INSECURITY YOU'VE SPENT THE LAST 10 YEARS TRYING TO OVERCOME. SEE YOU THERE! (OR ELSE WE'LL **REALLY** TALK!)..."

NICE TO SEE THEY HAVEN'T LOST THE OLD SCHOOL SPIRIT.
Guisewite

AT 5:32 I GOT AN INVITATION TO MY HIGH SCHOOL REUNION. AT 5:55 CONNIE KRAMER CALLED LONG DISTANCE AND BEGGED ME TO BE ON THE DECORATING COMMITTEE.

HOW DID THEY FIND YOU SO FAST? YOU DON'T LIVE IN THE SAME TOWN ANYMORE.

YOU DIDN'T STAY IN TOUCH WITH ANYONE FROM HIGH SCHOOL. HOW DID THEY EVEN KNOW WHERE YOU WERE?

PEOPLE NEVER LOSE TRACK OF WOMEN WHO KNOW HOW TO MAKE TISSUE PAPER FLOWERS.
Guisewite

LOOK AT ME IN MY HIGH SCHOOL YEARBOOK, ANDREA. WHAT A LOSER.
PEOPLE WHO FELT LIKE REJECTS IN HIGH SCHOOL OFTEN GO ON TO DO GREAT THINGS, CATHY.
MIDLAND HIGH SCHOOL

INSECURE PEOPLE ARE DRIVEN TO ACCOMPLISH MUCH MORE THAN PEOPLE WHO HAVE FELT COOL ALL THEIR LIVES.
MIDLAND HIGH SCHOOL

IT'S ALMOST LIKE THE WORSE YOU FELT ABOUT YOURSELF IN HIGH SCHOOL THE BETTER YOU'LL DO AS AN ADULT!
MIDLAND HIGH SCHOOL

JUST MY LUCK. I WASN'T A BIG ENOUGH LOSER.
Guisewite

THIS WAS MY BEST FRIEND IN HIGH SCHOOL. SHE GOT MARRIED. HERE'S MY OTHER BEST FRIEND. MARRIED.

THIS ONE GOT MARRIED, DIVORCED AND RE-MARRIED. THIS ONE'S MARRIED. LET'S SEE... MARRIED... MARRIED ... MARRIED... DIVORCED... MARRIED... MARRIED.

CATHY, THIS DOESN'T MAKE YOU FEEL BAD, DOES IT?
NO.. IT JUST MAKES ME REALIZE HOW DIFFERENT MY LIFE IS.

I'M GOING TO BE THE ONLY ONE AT MY HIGH SCHOOL REUNION WHO DOESN'T HAVE A FONDUE SET.
MIDLAND HIGH SCHOOL
Guisewite

THERE WERE TWO KINDS OF GIRLS IN HIGH SCHOOL... THE ONES WHO DANCED AND GOT CRAZY, AND THE ONES WHO RAN AROUND STICKING THE FLOWERS BACK ON THE FLOATS.

THAT WAS ME, ANDREA. CONSCIENTIOUS AND DATELESS. HO, HO! WAIT'LL MY GRADUATING CLASS SEES ME NOW!! HO, HO!!!

PEOPLE LIKE IT WHEN YOU'RE CONSISTENT.
Guisewite

I THOUGHT EVERYONE WAS SUPPOSED TO BE OLD AND FAT!!!

HI, CATHY. REMEMBER TOM?
SURE I REMEMBER YOU, TOM. 80% OF THE GIRLS IN OUR HIGH SCHOOL WASTED THEIR EDUCATIONS WRITING NOTES BACK AND FORTH ABOUT YOU.
CLASS REUNION

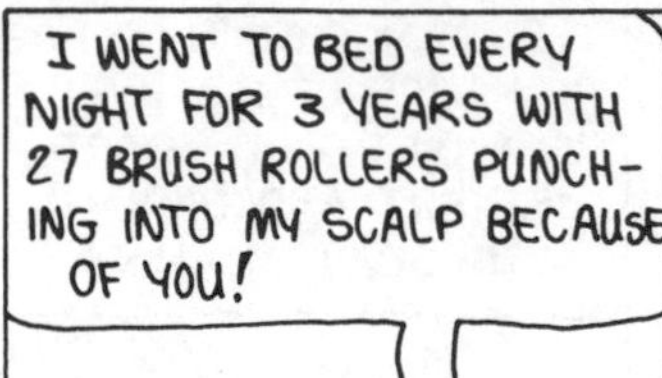
I WENT TO BED EVERY NIGHT FOR 3 YEARS WITH 27 BRUSH ROLLERS PUNCHING INTO MY SCALP BECAUSE OF YOU!

I WROTE YOUR NAME ALL OVER MY HISTORY NOTES, I DAYDREAMED THROUGH GEOMETRY AND I FLUNKED FRENCH BECAUSE OF YOU!!

HEY, CATHY... I'M SORRY.
HE SPOKE TO ME!
Guisewite

HI!
WELL, HI! HI, HOW ARE YOU??
MIDLAND HIGH CLASS REUNION
MHS

GREAT! GEE, IT'S BEEN SO LONG. WHAT ARE YOU DOING?
OH, THE SAME THING. YOU?
MHS

LITTLE OF THIS, LITTLE OF THAT. GOSH, IT'S GREAT TO SEE YOU!
I KNOW. I CAN'T BELIEVE IT! HA, HA! HERE WE ARE!!
MHS

...TWO PEOPLE WHO DON'T HAVE THE SLIGHTEST IDEA WHO THE OTHER ONE IS.
MHS
Guisewite

REMEMBER HOW WE USED TO SIT IN THIS GYM AND WHISPER ABOUT THE GUYS WE WANTED TO MEET?
YEAH... IT SEEMS LIKE A CENTURY AGO.
WELCOME CLASS REUNION

I KNOW. SINCE THEN I'VE BEEN THROUGH THE WHOLE ANTI-ESTABLISHMENT THING, THE ANTI-CAPITALIST THING, THE ANTI-MEN THING, THE ANTI-FAMILY THING, AND THE "ME!" THING...

I'VE GONE THROUGH 6 ALTERNATIVE LIFESTYLES, 17 RELATIONSHIPS, 9 RELIGIONS, 5 CAREERS, AND HERE WE ARE... BACK IN THE GYM IN PANTYHOSE AND PUMPS.
MHS

DO YOU RECOGNIZE THAT GUY OVER THERE?
NO... PRETTY CUTE, ISN'T HE?
MHS
Guisewite

THIS WOMAN NEVER SPOKE TO ME THE ENTIRE TIME WE WERE IN HIGH SCHOOL. SHE WAS TOO COOL.
"YAK YAK YAK YAK"

NOW SHE RAN OVER TO ME AND IS YAKKING AWAY LIKE SHE WAS MY BEST FRIEND.
"YAK YAK YAK"

"YAK YAK YAK YAK YAK YAK"

CELLULITE. THE GREAT EQUALIZER.
"YAK YAK YAK YAK YAK"

OF COURSE, YOU KNEW WHAT A CRUSH I HAD ON YOU IN HIGH SCHOOL, CATHY..
YOU HAD A CRUSH ON ME IN HIGH SCHOOL?
CLASS REUNION

EVERYONE IN THE WHOLE SCHOOL KNEW I HAD A CRUSH ON YOU.
I DIDN'T KNOW YOU HAD A CRUSH ON ME.

HOW COULD YOU NOT KNOW I HAD A CRUSH ON YOU?? THE ENTIRE WORLD KNEW I HAD A CRUSH ON YOU!!!

DO YOU STILL??

OH, CATHY! YOU'RE BACK FROM YOUR REUNION! TELL ME ALL ABOUT IT!
I SURVIVED, MOM.

I HAVE LOOKED MY PAST IN THE EYE, AND I'VE COME AWAY INTACT.

I LEFT THERE TOTALLY CONTENT WITH MY LIFE. I'M SATISFIED WITH MY ACCOMPLISHMENTS, AND I'M PROUD OF MYSELF AS A WOMAN AND A HUMAN BEING!!

COME ON, CATHY... ...GET TO THE GOOD STUFF.

DID THAT CUTE STEVE CLARK HAPPEN TO BE AT YOUR HIGH SCHOOL REUNION, CATHY ??
YEAH, MOM... WE TALKED ABOUT MARRIAGE.

MARRIAGE ?? OH, SWEETIE, STEVE IS SUCH A STABLE, LEVEL-HEADED YOUNG MAN!

MARRIAGE WITH STEVE WOULD BE A REAL LIFE-TIME COMMITMENT! MARRIAGE WITH STEVE WOULD BE FOREVER !!

WE TALKED ABOUT HIS MARRIAGE TO SUSAN.
MAYBE IT WON'T WORK OUT.

HOW ABOUT SOME DINNER, CATHY ?
SURE, IRVING.
SEPTEMBER 1981

HERE YOU GO.
BREAD

DINNER USED TO LAST LONGER WHEN MY MOTHER COOKED IT.

YOUR OFFICE SAID YOU WEREN'T IN TODAY, CATHY. YOU AREN'T SICK, ARE YOU ?
NO, MOM. I SPENT THE DAY IN ST. LOUIS.

ST. LOUIS ?? MY WORD! YOU FLEW ALL THE WAY TO ST. LOUIS TODAY ??
YES. I GOT UP AT 5:00, CAUGHT A 6:30 PLANE...

... SPENT THE DAY AT A MANAGEMENT SEMINAR, HAD DINNER WITH A CLIENT, AND JUST GOT HOME A FEW MINUTES AGO.

DID YOU HAVE A CHANCE TO STOP IN ON YOUR AUNT DOROTHY ?

GOODNIGHT...THIS IS SILLY. I CAN'T SEEM TO HANG UP.
I KNOW, BUT WE HAVE TO. IT'S LONG DISTANCE AND IT'S COSTING A FORTUNE. GOODNIGHT.

MAYBE DAVID LOST MY PHONE NUMBER, ANDREA...
MEN DON'T LOSE WOMEN'S PHONE NUMBERS, CATHY.

THEY THROW THEM ALL ONTO LITTLE TRAYS ON TOP OF THEIR DRESSERS. THEN WHEN MEN GET BORED, THEY FISH THROUGH THE TRAY AND PULL OUT A LUCKY WINNER AND THAT'S WHO THEY CALL.

THAT'S WHO THEY CALL, WHO THEY DATE, WHO THEY MARRY, WHO THEY GET PREGNANT, WHO THEY DIVORCE, AND WHO THEY DON'T PAY ANY ALIMONY TO!!

HI, CATHY. IT'S DAVID.
WHAT DO **YOU** WANT?!!

WHERE IS EVERYONE? WE'RE SUPPOSED TO HAVE A MEETING AT 8:30.

MR. PINKLEY, PLEASE COME IN HERE. LEE, WILL YOU AND BETTY QUIT WAITING FOR EVERYONE ELSE TO COME TO THE MEETING BEFORE YOU DO??

NO, ALAN, YOU MAY **NOT** RUN OUT TO WARM UP YOUR COFFEE! NO ONE IS LEAVING THIS ROOM UNTIL... GET BACK IN HERE, JOHN!

TIRED?
I'M EXHAUSTED. I SPENT THE WHOLE MORNING ALMOST IN A MEETING.

I HAVEN'T LEFT THE APARTMENT FOR 6 HOURS BECAUSE DAVID SAID HE'D CALL AND I KNOW THAT SOMETIMES HIS BUSINESS GETS IN THE WAY, JUST LIKE MINE DOES.

I'M WAITING FOR HIM TO CALL INSTEAD OF ME CALLING HIM BECAUSE I KNOW WHAT I HAVE TO OFFER, AND HE'D BE A FOOL IF HE DIDN'T RECOGNIZE IT.

NOW I'M EATING A ONE-POUND BAG OF M&M'S BECAUSE I NO LONGER FEEL I HAVE TO BE A SIZE 3 TO BE A VIABLE, ATTRACTIVE MEMBER OF SOCIETY.
M&M's

I'M DOING ALL THE WRONG THINGS FOR ALL THE RIGHT REASONS.
Guisewite

THAT WAS KAREN. HER BOYFRIEND DUMPED HER, SHE GOT MAD, STARTED HER OWN BUSINESS AND JUST GROSSED $500,000.00 IN SALES.

JOAN WENT TO HAWAII TO RECOVER FROM BEING FIRED, LANDED A REAL ESTATE DEAL, AND IS MANAGING HER OWN STRING OF CONDOMINIUMS ON THE BEACH.

PAULA GOT FAT, FOUNDED A WEIGHT LOSS CLINIC, LOST 53 POUNDS, AND FELL IN LOVE WITH THE MOST HANDSOME MAN I'VE EVER SEEN IN MY LIFE.

EVERYONE I KNOW IS HAVING A MORE PRODUCTIVE CRISIS THAN I AM.

WHAT A GREAT MOVIE! I LOVED THAT MOVIE, IRVING.
YEAH, ME TOO.
NOW SHOWING
BODY HEAT

OH, IRVING...PLEASE DON'T JUMP IN THE CAR AND TURN THE RADIO ON LIKE YOU USUALLY DO, OKAY?
HUH?
BODY HEAT

I WANT THIS MOVIE TO LAST IN MY HEAD AND WHEN YOU TURN THE RADIO ON IT BREAKS THE WHOLE SPELL.
WE'RE NOT EVEN IN THE PARKING LOT YET! MAYBE I WASN'T GOING TO TURN THE RADIO ON!!

TURN THE RADIO ON, IRVING.
MOVIE
ARKING

SHOULD I TELL IRVING ABOUT DAVID OR NOT, ANDREA? I DON'T KNOW WHAT TO DO.

I GUESS I SHOULD TELL HIM. NO. THAT WOULD BE STUPID. I'LL WAIT AND SEE WHAT HAPPENS. THEN I'LL TELL HIM.

NO. I'LL TELL HIM RIGHT NOW. NO. I DON'T KNOW. SHOULD I TELL HIM OR SHOULDN'T I TELL HIM??
COOKIES

WHAT DOES THE LITTLE VOICE INSIDE YOU SAY?
EAT EAT EAT EAT
COOKIES

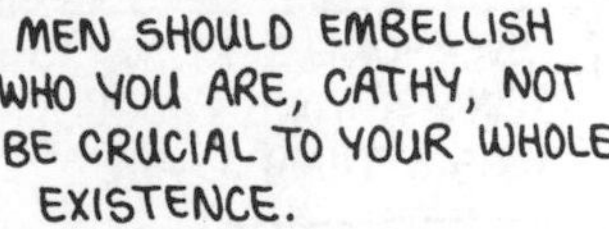
MEN SHOULD EMBELLISH WHO YOU ARE, CATHY, NOT BE CRUCIAL TO YOUR WHOLE EXISTENCE.

MEN SHOULD BE A COMPLEMENT TO YOUR LIFE, NOT A NECESSITY.

MEN ARE SORT OF LIKE POTATO CHIP DIP.

SINCE WHEN IS POTATO CHIP DIP NOT A NECESSITY ??!

IS THAT MY PHONE ? I HAVE TO GET MY PHONE !
EH, LET IT RING.

IRVING, MY PHONE IS RING-ING ! I HAVE TO GET MY PHONE !

WHAT FOR? YOUR SWEETHEART IS RIGHT HERE, CATHY.

WAIT A MINUTE... ARE YOU WAITING FOR SOME OTHER GUY TO CALL OR WHAT ??
YES, IRVING. YES, I MET ANOTHER MAN AND I'M NOT GOING TO MISS MY ONE CHANCE ALL WEEK TO TALK TO HIM !!!

THIS HAD BETTER BE IMPORTANT, MOTHER.

ARE YOU GOING TO GO VISIT DAVID IN ST. LOUIS OR NOT, CATHY ?
I DON'T KNOW, ANDREA.

ON ONE HAND, I ONLY HAVE ONE LIFE TO LIVE.. ...AND WHY NOT ??

ON THE OTHER HAND, I COULD BE RISKING EVERY-THING I'VE BUILT WITH IRVING IF HE FINDS OUT.

HOW ABOUT IF I GO BUT I DON'T HAVE A GOOD TIME ?

OF COURSE YOUR MOTHER WOULD BE UPSET IF YOU TOLD HER YOU WERE RUNNING OFF TO SPEND A WEEKEND IN ST. LOUIS WITH A MAN YOU BARELY KNOW.

WHY DO YOU NEED TO TELL HER ? I KNOW WHY... APPROVAL. IF SHE KNOWS, YOU CAN SOMEHOW PUT THE WHOLE BURDEN FOR WHATEVER HAPPENS ON HER.

YOU'RE NOT TELLING YOUR MOTHER TO BE HONEST, CATHY... YOU'RE TELLING HER SO YOU WON'T FEEL SO GUILTY !!

SOUNDS GOOD TO ME.

WHAT ARE YOU TAKING TO ST. LOUIS ?
WELL, DAVID SAID WE MIGHT PLAY A LITTLE TENNIS.

THEN I THOUGHT WE'D HAVE A ROMANTIC PICNIC IN THE PARK, SEE A BEAUTIFUL, SENSITIVE COMEDY, HAVE DINNER IN A CHARMING FRENCH RESTAURANT, LAUGH, TALK...

...DANCE UNDER THE STARS, AND FALL SO TOTALLY IN LOVE WITH EACH OTHER THAT DAVID WOULD BEG ME TO STAY FOR FOUR MONTHS.

HOPE FILLS UP A LOT OF SUITCASES.

EXCUSE ME... I'M VERY SORRY... THIS IS THE LAST TIME I'LL BOTHER YOU.
YOU MUST BE GOING TO SEE SOMEONE VERY SPECIAL.

WELL, YES. YES I AM! I GUESS IT SHOWS.
YES, IT SHOWS.

PLUS THE FACT THAT EVERY TIME YOU COME BACK FROM THE LADIES ROOM YOUR COLOGNE IS A LITTLE BIT STRONGER AND NOW I CAN HARDLY BREATHE.

EXCUSE ME... I BEG YOUR PARDON...

CALL ME UP, DAVID! PLEASE CALL AND TELL ME HOW MUCH YOU ENJOYED LAST WEEKEND!
DING DONG!

CATHY, HONEY, I HAD TO SEE YOU.
IRVING! IRVING... ..UH, JUST A MINUTE..

I CHANGED MY MIND, DAVID! WAIT! DON'T CALL NOW! NO! SHHH! DON'T CALL NOW!
RING RING

AHEM... SORRY, IRVING. I'M ON THE PHONE.
RING
RING
RING
RING
Guisewite

WHAT SHOULD I TELL IRVING ABOUT MY VISIT TO DAVID?
WHY DO YOU HAVE TO TELL HIM ANY-THING?

WELL, WHAT ARE WE GOING TO TALK ABOUT? ANDREA, THIS IS IMPORTANT!

I HAVE OPENED ANOTHER DOOR IN MY LIFE AND I DON'T KNOW WHAT TO SAY TO HIM ANYMORE!!
WHAT DID YOU SAY WHEN YOU OPENED YOUR LAST DOOR?

EXCUSE THE MESS.
Guisewite

DAVID SAID HE WAS DOING LAUNDRY TONIGHT... I WONDER IF HE REMEMBERS WE USED UP ALL THE DETERGENT LAST WEEKEND.

WE USED UP ALL HIS COFFEE, TOO... OH, AND I WAS GOING TO REMIND HIM I PUT HIS LAST ONION AND BIT OF VINEGAR IN THE SALAD.

I FEEL SO CLOSE TO HIM, ANDREA.
Guisewite

I KNOW EVERYTHING HE'S OUT OF.

OKAY, WHERE'S THE PAIR OF PANTYHOSE WITHOUT THE RUN? I KNOW YOU'RE IN HERE.

COME OUT THIS SECOND! PLEASE! I PROMISE I WILL NEVER DUMP OLD PANTYHOSE IN THIS DRAWER AGAIN!!

...AHAH!
DUMP!

I HAVE TO RUN OUT AND GET SOME LUNCH, CHARLENE. I'M STARVING!

WHY DON'T YOU JUST GET SOMETHING FROM THE VENDING MACHINES?
BLEAH! ALL THEY HAVE IS DISGUSTING JUNK FOOD IN THOSE MACHINES.

I PREFER TO BUY MY DISGUSTING JUNK FOOD IN A RESTAURANT.

I WANT TO KNOW EVERYTHING ABOUT YOU, CATHY.
OH, DAVID, I'VE ALREADY TOLD YOU SO MUCH! WE'VE BEEN ON THE PHONE FOR TWO HOURS!

TELL ME MORE, CATHY. I WANT TO KNOW HOW YOU FEEL ABOUT EVERYTHING.

COME ON, CATHY... YOU DON'T HAVE TO BE AFRAID TO SAY ANYTHING TO ME.
I'M NOT AFRAID.

THEN WHY THE BIG PAUSES?
I'M STARTING TO HAVE TO MAKE THINGS UP.

HI, CATHY.

OH, MOM! IT'S **YOU**! I LOVE YOU! I'M SO HAPPY YOU CALLED! HOW **ARE YOU**?!

...WAIT. I CAN'T READ THAT TO MY MOTHER...ACK.. SHE'D DIE IF SHE HEARD THAT...I CAN'T TELL HER THAT...

THIS IS AN EMERGENCY, CATHY! CAN YOU HELP ME OUT??
NO, MR. PINKLEY. NO, I CANNOT.

I HAVE LUNCH PLANS TODAY, AND FOR ONCE I'M GOING TO KEEP THEM!!

THIS IS AN EMERGENCY, CATHY! CAN YOU HELP ME OUT??
SURE.

IT'S HARD TO KEEP THE MOMENTUM GOING.
Guisewite

OH, CATHY, YOU'RE BACK. I WAS JUST ABOUT TO LEAVE A NOTE.
SORRY, MOM. I RAN OUT FOR A HAMBURGER.

FIRST THERE WEREN'T ANY PARKING SPOTS, THEN THERE WAS A HUGE LINE, THEN IT TOOK THEM FOREVER TO MAKE A HAMBURGER WITH NO PICKLES ON IT.

WHY DIDN'T YOU JUST MAKE ONE OF THESE NICE PACKAGES OF SOUP FOR YOURSELF?

I DIDN'T WANT TO WAIT THE THREE MINUTES FOR THE WATER TO HEAT UP.
Guisewite

DID YOU TELL IRVING ABOUT DAVID YET?
NO. I DECIDED TO GIVE IRVING ONE LAST CHANCE.

I'M GOING TO GO OUT WITH HIM TONIGHT AND REALLY WATCH WITH THE OLD CRITICAL EYE.

I'M GOING TO PAY ATTENTION TO EVERY WORD AND GESTURE. I'M GOING TO EVALUATE, COMPARE, AND COME TO SOME REAL CONCLUSIONS ABOUT OUR FUTURE!

HI, CATHY.
YOU SEEM A LITTLE RELAXED FOR ALL THE PRESSURE YOU'RE UNDER TONIGHT.
Guisewite

IN WORLD NEWS TONIGHT OFFICIALS AT THE WHITE HOUSE SAY...
CATHY...
SHHH!

CATHY, YOU LOOK BEAUTIFUL TONIGHT. I...
WILL YOU BE QUIET? I'M TRYING TO WATCH THE NEWS!!

SORRY, IRVING.. I HAVEN'T BEEN ON A DATE IN AWHILE.

HERE I AM HAVING DINNER WITH IRVING AND ALL I CAN THINK ABOUT IS DAVID.

WHO AM I KIDDING? IRVING'S PROBABLY SITTING THERE THINKING ABOUT THE WOMAN HE WENT OUT WITH LAST WEEKEND.

HOW ROMANTIC. IT'S JUST THE FOUR OF US.

DAVID SAID HE MISSED ME...
FORGET DAVID. WHAT'S FOR LUNCH?

I WONDER IF I TURNED THE COFFEE POT OFF?
IRVING SAID HE'D...
YAAA! I FORGOT THE DRAPE REPORT...

MY EXPENSE REPORTS ARE...
SHAMPOO.. MILK...
WAIT. ANDREA HAS MY...
BANK!
FIND THE ARTEX MEMO...
ASK MOM TO ...
CALL TOM.
WAIT, I LEFT...
THE SOCKS...

CATHY!!
SORRY, MR. PINKLEY. I THINK MY CONTROLLERS ARE ON STRIKE.

THESE STRETCH JEANS ARE THE LATEST THING. THEY GIVE THAT DESIGNER FIT, YET LET YOU BREATHE AND MOVE FREELY.
WHY, THANK YOU. I'D LOVE TO TRY A PAIR.
STRETCH JEANS

YAAAAA!

CRASH!
RIP!
SQUASH!
CRASH!

DID YOU WANT THOSE?
Guisewite

ARE YOU OKAY, DAVID?
I'M FINE, CATHY. ARE YOU OKAY?

SURE, I'M OKAY. DO YOU FEEL DIFFERENT ABOUT ANYTHING?
NO. NO, NOTHING'S DIFFERENT. EVERYTHING'S FINE.

OKAY. WELL, I'M FINE TOO. UM, GOODNIGHT.
GOODNIGHT.

ABSENCE MAKES THE HEART GROW WEIRDER.
Guisewite

IT'S FREEZING IN HERE!
I KNOW. I WENT AND GOT ALL MY WINTER CLOTHES OUT OF STORAGE LAST WEEK.

DID YOU GET YOUR WINTER CLOTHES OUT OF STORAGE YET, CATHY?

YES.
Guisewite

DAVID! WHAT ARE **YOU** DOING IN TOWN?? I...
HELLO, BEAUTIFUL... AND YOU MUST BE IRVING. I'VE HEARD SO MUCH ABOUT YOU.

I HAVE ONLY THE GREATEST RESPECT FOR YOUR RELATIONSHIP WITH CATHY, IRVING... ...BUT I FIND MYSELF IN THE AWKWARD POSITION OF WANTING TO SPEND TIME WITH HER, TOO.

I HOPED THAT IF WE COULD TALK THIS OVER IN PERSON, IT MIGHT MAKE THINGS LESS UNCOMFORTABLE FOR EVERYONE. CAN I BUY YOU A DRINK, IRVING?
WHAT THE HECK?

Guisewite

HOW DID YOU FEEL WHEN I CAME OVER TO CATHY'S AND TOLD YOU HOW MUCH I WANTED TO GO OUT WITH HER?
I FELT LIKE PUNCHING YOUR FACE IN.

YEAH, WELL... I GUESS WE'VE ALL BEEN THERE. BY SMASHING SOMEONE'S FACE YOU RELIEVE THE TENSION WITHOUT HAVING TO ADMIT THAT YOU FEEL HURT.

IT'S JUST CONDITIONING, IRVING. WE ALL BOUGHT IT. THEY TAUGHT US IT WAS MORE MANLY TO ACT LIKE 6-YEAR-OLDS THAN TO TALK ABOUT HOW WE FEEL.

NOW I REALLY FEEL LIKE PUNCHING YOUR FACE IN.

I'VE COME TO SHOW YOU ST. LOUIS IN THE FALL! OUR PLANE LEAVES IN AN HOUR.
AN **HOUR**? DAVID, WHAT ABOUT WORK? WHAT ABOUT IRVING??

CATHY, IF WE WAIT FOR EVERYTHING TO BE CONVENIENT, WE'RE GOING TO MISS ANY CHANCE WE EVER HAD.
PLANE

YOU CAN DO THIS... JUST ONCE, STOP YOUR LIFE IN ITS TRACKS, LOOK THE WORLD IN THE EYE AND SAY, "**I'M** IN CHARGE! THE NEXT THREE DAYS BELONG TO **ME**!!"

EVERY TIME I TAKE CHARGE OF MY OWN LIFE SOMEBODY ELSE IS HOLDING THE TICKET.
Guisewite

I APOLOGIZE FOR THE LACK OF WARNING, MR. PINKLEY, BUT I MUST TAKE A FEW PERSONAL DAYS OFF STARTING TODAY.

CHARLENE IS COVERING ON THE KLINE PROJECT. ALAN IS TAKING CARE OF THE RILEY ACCOUNT. AND I ASKED JILL TO LOOK OVER THE BRADLEY FIGURES...AM I FORGETTING ANYTHING ?

THE HOSTESS HO-HO'S ARE IN MY BOTTOM RIGHT HAND DRAWER.
Guisewite

MMMM...
I HAVEN'T HAD ONE OF THESE IN YEARS!

HERE, TRY THIS ONE, DAVID!
OOH... MY FAVORITE!
TRICK OR TREAT

YAAAA!
Guisewite

CATHY, WHEN YOU SAY "I DON'T KNOW WHAT I WANT FOR LUNCH" WHAT YOU'RE REALLY THINKING IS "I DON'T KNOW WHAT YOU WANT FOR LUNCH."

YOU'LL NEVER MAKE DECISIONS IN OUR RELATIONSHIP IF YOU TRY TO SECOND GUESS ME ALL THE TIME.

I WANT YOU TO BE AN EQUAL VOICE IN EVERYTHING WE DO. DON'T THINK ABOUT ME... JUST SAY WHAT YOU WANT FOR LUNCH!!

GIVE ME A HINT.
Guisewite

CATHY STILL ISN'T HOME. WHERE IS SHE ??

MAYBE SHE'S AT HOME BUT SHE ISN'T ANSWERING THE PHONE BECAUSE SHE'S AVOIDING ME.

MAYBE SHE KNOWS IT'S ME CALLING AND SHE'S JUST SITTING THERE COUNTING THE NUMBER OF TIMES I LET IT RING... THAT'S DISGUSTING!

THAT'S EXACTLY THE SORT OF THING **I'D** DO!!
Guisewite

WELL?? HOW WAS YOUR LITTLE "**EMERGENCY VACATION**", CATHY ??
I KNOW YOU LIKE TO GET THE NEWS FIRST, CHARLENE. SO HERE IT IS...

I SPENT FOUR GLORIOUS DAYS RUNNING ALL OVER ST. LOUIS WITH AN INCREDIBLY HANDSOME MAN!

YOU TOOK FOUR DAYS OFF WORK AND YOU WEREN'T SNEAKING AROUND HAVING INTERVIEWS?! WHAT'S THE MATTER WITH YOU??!

FORGET IT, EVERYBODY. SHE WAS JUST OFF SEEING SOME GUY.
Guisewite

RINSE RINSE
WAIT A MINUTE. DID I USE THE CONDITIONER YET OR NOT?

I MUST STILL BE HALF ASLEEP. I CAN'T REMEMBER

I CAN'T TELL FROM THE BOTTLE... I CAN'T TELL FROM MY HAIR... EH, I MUST HAVE USED CONDITIONER.

SEASON'S GREETINGS TO YOU, TOO, CHARLENE.
Guisewite

WILL HE STILL LOVE ME AFTER HE GETS HIS PHONE BILL?

WHY DON'T I KNOW WHAT'S GOING ON?!

IN
OUT
CATHY

IN
OUT
CATHY

I LOVE THE FALL.
Guisewite

IT'S HARD WHEN YOU'RE THE ONE WHO ENDS A RELATIONSHIP, CATHY... YOU QUIT THINKING ABOUT THE MAN AS THE ONE YOU DUMPED AND START THINKING ABOUT HIM AS **A** MAN WHO GOT DUMPED **ON**.

YOU GET SYMPATHETIC. YOU REACH OUT TO COMFORT AND CONSOLE...

...AND SUDDENLY, YOU'RE BACK ON THE COUCH TELLING JOKES AND EATING DORRITOS WITH THE GUY YOU WERE NEVER GOING TO SPEAK TO AGAIN.

ANDREA HAS THE LIVING ROOM BUGGED.
Guisewite

YOU WENT OUT AND GOT DRUNK BECAUSE YOU WERE JEALOUS? THAT WAS STUPID.
HOW IS THAT ANY MORE STUPID THAN YOU **EATING** WHEN YOU'RE JEALOUS?

IRVING, I EAT WHEN I'M **DEPRESSED**. I BUY **SHOES** WHEN I'M JEALOUS. I BREAK THE TELEPHONE WHEN I'M ANGRY...

I MANGLE MY FINGERNAILS WHEN I'M LONELY... I THROW THINGS ALL OVER THE HOUSE WHEN I'M HURT... AND I WASTE MONEY ON MAKE-UP WHEN I'M FRUSTRATED.

MEN JUST DON'T KNOW HOW TO COPE.
Guisewite

DAVID'S COMING TO TOWN THIS WEEKEND, MOM!
OH? THE SAME DAVID WHO NEVER CALLS WHEN HE SAYS?

THAT HAPPENED ONE TIME. HE'S A WONDERFUL MAN.
WELL, I'M SURE HE ISN'T AS NICE AS IRVING.

IRVING ALWAYS CALLS WHEN HE SAYS. IRVING IS "KIND, BRILLIANT, THOUGHTFUL, GENEROUS, PERFECT, LOVES CHILDREN AND IS A POTENTIAL MILLIONAIRE!"

I MAY HAVE GIVEN YOU TOO BIG A BUILD-UP ON IRVING, MOM.
Guisewite

AHAH! I KNEW IT! I KNEW YOU'D BE AT CATHY'S IF I CAME OVER!!
YES, IRVING, YOU PROBABLY DID.

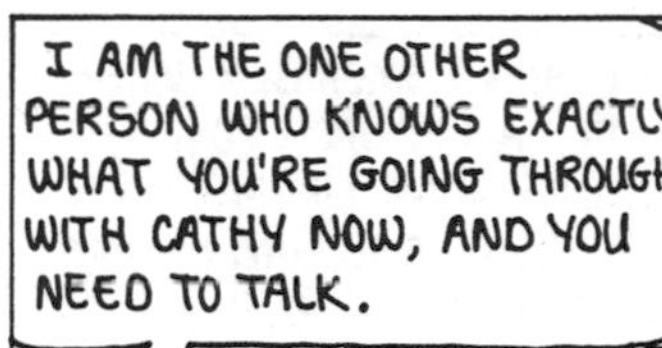
I AM THE ONE OTHER PERSON WHO KNOWS EXACTLY WHAT YOU'RE GOING THROUGH WITH CATHY NOW, AND YOU NEED TO TALK.

I ADMIRE YOU FOR BEING ABLE TO OPEN UP AND SHARE LIKE THIS, IRVING.
WHERE'S CATHY?

TO US.
Guisewite

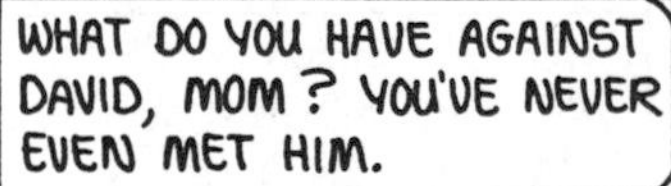
WHAT DO YOU HAVE AGAINST DAVID, MOM? YOU'VE NEVER EVEN MET HIM.

CATHY, YOUR FATHER AND I HAVE FINALLY ACCEPTED IRVING.

BRING DAVID INTO THE PICTURE, AND SUDDENLY WE HAVE TO START ALL OVER MAKING CHIT-CHAT WITH SOME STRANGER.

WHAT WILL WE WEAR? WHAT WILL WE SAY? WHAT IF HE DOESN'T LIKE US??
MOM, I'M THE ONE HE'S DATING.

WHEN YOU DATE, WE ALL DATE.
Guisewite

IRVING, YOU LOOK SO CUTE IN YOUR NECKTIE!

DAVID, YOU'RE JUST ADORABLE!

WELL, I GUESS I DON'T HAVE TO SAY WHAT ONE BIG QUESTION IS ON ALL OF OUR MINDS TODAY!!!

ARE YOU GOING TO BE LIKE YOUR MOTHER WHEN YOU'RE HER AGE?

IRVING'S RECORDS... IRVING'S BOOKS... IRVING'S TENNIS RACKET... IRVING'S BARBEQUE AND SOCKS.

JUST CALL IRVING AND TELL HIM TO COME GET HIS THINGS SO YOU CAN GET ON WITH YOUR LIFE.
ANDREA, I'M NOT READY TO GO THROUGH THIS ORDEAL.

IT'S NO ORDEAL. IT'S EASY. IT'S EFFICIENT. THE WHOLE THING WILL TAKE FIVE MINUTES!
THAT'S THE SAME THING YOU TOLD ME ABOUT PUTTING UP CURTAIN RODS.

I DON'T SEE MY WOOL PLAID SHIRT IN THESE THINGS YOU'RE RETURNING.
I WAS HOPING YOU WOULD WANT ME TO KEEP THAT SHIRT, IRVING.

FOR WHAT? A SOUVENIR??
IRVING, WHEN COUPLES SEPARATE, THE MAN OFTEN LEAVES ONE FAVORITE SHIRT, SORT OF AS...

AAAAA! DON'T TAKE THE WOOL PLAID SHIRT!

SO MUCH FOR THE ROMANCE OF BREAKING UP.

I GAVE IRVING ALL OF HIS RECORDS AND BOOKS BACK, DAVID.

I GAVE HIM THE LAMP WE FOUND TOGETHER AT A GARAGE SALE AND THE PLASTIC MUG I WON FOR HIM AT THE FAIR. I EVEN GAVE HIM BACK HIS WOOL PLAID SHIRT.

I HAD HIM TAKE EVERYTHING AWAY SO I COULD MAKE ROOM IN MY LIFE FOR YOU.
OH, CATHY...

DON'T COME NEAR ME!!

I SHOULDN'T OPEN THIS BOX OF COOKIES. EH, SO WHAT ?
COOKIES

SO WHAT ? I DON'T CARE.

I DON'T CARE AND I DON'T CARE **WHY** I DON'T CARE !! **HA! I JUST DON'T CARE** !!
COOKIES

CATHY, WHAT HAPPENED IN HERE ??
MY LIVING ROOM AND I WENT OFF OUR DIET.
Guisewite

EXCUSE ME...DO YOU KNOW ANYTHING ABOUT PICKING WINE ?
CERTAINLY. FIRST YOU ELIMINATE THE MOST AND LEAST EXPENSIVE.

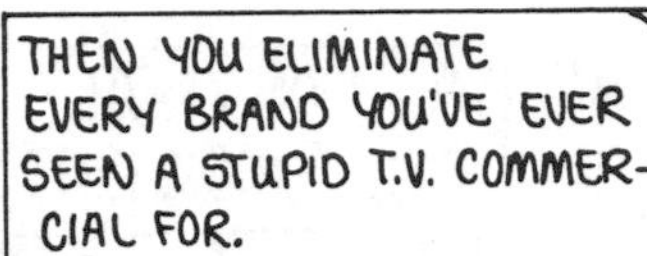
THEN YOU ELIMINATE EVERY BRAND YOU'VE EVER SEEN A STUPID T.V. COMMERCIAL FOR.

THEN YOU ELIMINATE ANY WINERY THAT STARTS WITH THE FIRST INITIAL OF THE LAST MAN YOU HAD A FIGHT WITH.

THEN YOU GO "EENY-MEENY-MINEY-MOE" DOWN THE REMAINING SELECTIONS... ...AND VOILÁ !
I KNEW THAT !
Guisewite

I KNOW. I'M SORRY I'M LATE.
WHAT HAPPENED ? DID YOU FORGET TO SET YOUR ALARM ?

I MOST CERTAINLY DID NOT. MR. PINKLEY, I HAPPEN TO BE ONE OF YOUR MOST RESPONSIBLE EMPLOYEES.

I'M CONSCIENTIOUS, THOROUGH, AND HAVE A HIGH RESPECT FOR OFFICE HOURS.
WHY DIDN'T YOU GET UP WHEN YOUR ALARM WENT OFF ?

IT WAS DARK OUT !!
Guisewite

MAY I HELP YOU?
YES. I NEED SOME QUICK GIFT IDEAS FOR MY BOYFRIEND... HE'S RIGHT AROUND THE CORNER.

CERTAINLY. WHAT'S HE LIKE?
OH, HE'S GORGEOUS, BRILLIANT, FUNNY, KIND, CARING, SWEET, AMBITIOUS...

MAY I HELP YOU?
Guisewite

WHAT DO YOU WANT FOR CHRISTMAS, MOM?
OH, LET'S SEE...
GIFTS
CHRISTMA COOKWAR SALE

I'D LIKE YOU TO GET BACK TOGETHER WITH THE YOUNG MEN YOU ALIENATED OVER THANKSGIVING, AND FOR ONE OF THEM TO GIVE YOU A GREAT BIG DIAMOND RING IN A VELVET BOX.

THEN YOU'LL GET MARRIED, HAVE A BABY, AND START WEARING PRETTY HATS LIKE PRINCESS DIANA AND LIVE HAPPILY EVER AFTER IN A BEAUTIFUL CASTLE!!

CAN I HELP YOU?
I DON'T THINK SO.
Guisewite

THIS BLOUSE WILL MAKE A WONDERFUL GIFT.
YES, I THOUGHT SO.
SAVE

IT'S SUCH A PRETTY, NEUTRAL COLOR. IT WILL GO WITH EVERYTHING. GOOD CHOICE!
THANK YOU.

OH, LOOK. IT'S WASHABLE! IT'S SO UNUSUAL TO FIND A BLOUSE THIS PRETTY THAT'S WASHABLE!

WHERE'S THE BLOUSE YOU BOUGHT, CATHY?
I GAVE IT TO THE SALES CLERK.
Guisewite

WHAT'S ALL THIS??
MY DESK WAS CLEAN WHEN I LEFT ON FRIDAY!
PINKLEY

WHERE DID ALL THIS COME FROM? I KNOW I FILED EVERYTHING LAST WEEK.
CHARLENE

WHAT'S GOING ON HERE??
WHO PUT ALL THIS JUNK ON MY DESK??
IN
OUT
CATHY

..NOBODY LIKES IT WHEN YOU SPEND THE WEEKEND IN THE OFFICE, MORRIS.
MORRIS

WHEN CAN WE DO SOME SHOPPING TOGETHER, CATHY?
I DON'T KNOW, ANDREA. TONIGHT IS KAY'S CHRISTMAS PARTY...

WEDNESDAY IS THE DALE'S CHRISTMAS PARTY... THURSDAY IS THE OFFICE CHRISTMAS PARTY...

...AND FRIDAY IS THE APARTMENT BUILDING PARTY!

WHAT ARE YOU DOING ON SATURDAY?
HAVING MY JAWS WIRED SHUT.

WHY ARE YOU TAKING **IRVING** TO YOUR OFFICE PARTY??
I KNOW THE TROUBLE A SINGLE WOMAN CAN HAVE AT AN OFFICE CHRISTMAS PARTY, ANDREA.

IRVING WILL NOT ONLY PROTECT ME FROM THE ADVANCES OF DRUNKEN EMPLOYEES...

...HIS PRESENCE WILL KEEP THE SPOUSES FROM FEELING THREATENED BY ME AS AN ATTRACTIVE, AVAILABLE MEMBER OF THE CORPORATE FAMILY.

MR. PINKLEY? JOANNE? OKAY... I THINK WE'RE FINALLY ALL HERE.
1981

WE HAVE MANY IMPORTANT THINGS ON OUR AGENDA TODAY, SO LET'S NOT WASTE ANY MORE TIME.
1981

ALL THOSE IN FAVOR OF **NOT** HOLDING OUR OFFICE CHRISTMAS PARTY ON A WEEK NIGHT NEXT YEAR, SAY "AYE".
Guisewite

THESE CHRISTMAS CARDS ARE FOR MY BUSINESS FRIENDS WHO CHANGED JOBS AND I CAN'T REMEMBER WHERE THEY WORK NOW.

Christmas
cards

THESE ARE FOR MY PERSONAL FRIENDS WHO MOVED LAST YEAR AND I CAN'T FIND THEIR NEW ADDRESSES.
christmas

THESE ARE FOR MY FRIENDS WHO EITHER GOT MARRIED OR DIVORCED AND NOBODY KNOWS WHAT NAME THEY'RE GOING BY ANYMORE.

I NEVER REALIZED HOW STABLE I WAS BEFORE.
Christmas
cards
Guisewite

THAT SIMPLE DRESS CAN BECOME AN ENTIRE WARDROBE OF GREAT HOLIDAY LOOKS.
THIS?
Holiday Special

SEE? YOU CAN BELT IT, BLOUSE IT, WRAP IT, LAYER IT, TUNIC IT, SASH IT, TUCK IT...

THE VARIETIES ARE ENDLESS! HARD TO BELIEVE, ISN'T IT?!!
3

YES. WITH JUST ONE DRESS, I HAVE LOOKED TERRIBLE IN 23 DIFFERENT OUTFITS.
Guisewite

HOW ABOUT SOME KITCHEN-WARE FOR YOUR DAUGHTER?
OH, NO. CATHY WILL THINK I'M MAKING AN ISSUE OF THE FACT THAT SHE ISN'T MARRIED YET AND SHOULD ALREADY HAVE ALL THAT STUFF.

HOW ABOUT SOMETHING FOR HER OFFICE?
NO. SHE'LL THINK I'M PURPOSELY AVOIDING ANYTHING TO DO WITH HER CHAOTIC HOME LIFE.

HOW ABOUT SOMETHING TO WEAR?
HEAVENS NO. SHE'LL THINK I'M ATTACKING THE RIDICULOUS GET-UPS SHE SPENDS HER MONEY ON.
HOLIDAY WEAR

IT'S IMPOSSIBLE TO SHOP FOR SOMEONE WHO'S SO CRITICAL!
Guisewite

HEY, CATHY! WHAT ARE YOU DOING IN THE MEN'S SECTION?
JUST BROWSING.
WANT ME TO **RING THAT UP** NOW?

YOU'RE NOT SPENDING MONEY ON IRVING, ARE YOU?
DON'T BE SILLY.
IRVING'S GOING TO LOVE THIS!!

CATHY, HOW **COULD** YOU??
IT'S CHEAP, ANDREA. IT'S VERY CHEAP.
THAT'LL BE $45.95! **YOUR TOTAL IS $45.95!!**

I HAVE TO DO **SOMETHING** TO MAKE MY JOB INTERESTING.
Guisewite

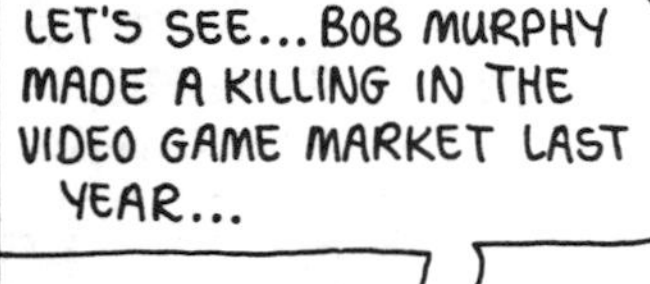
LET'S SEE... BOB MURPHY MADE A KILLING IN THE VIDEO GAME MARKET LAST YEAR...

Christmas Cards
Merry Merry Christmas

HIS WIFE BETSY OPENED HER OWN FRANCHISED CHAIN OF CREPE SHOPS... LITTLE SUSIE MURPHY GOT HER DOCTORATE AND HAD TWINS...
Christmas Cards

...BOTH OF WHOM SPEAK FLUENT FRENCH AT 8 MONTHS. ......ISN'T THAT WONDERFUL?! NOW, WHO'S READY FOR SOME MORE PIE?
Christmas Cards

Merry Merry Christmas

IF IRVING SEES ME LIKE THIS, HE'LL THINK I GOT ALL DRESSED UP BECAUSE I MISSED HIM.

HAH! I HAVE TO LOOK ALOOF! CASUAL, GRUBBY AND ALOOF!

HI, CATHY. MERRY CHRISTMAS!

OH, IRVING... YOU MISSED ME TOO!

WHAT ARE YOU DOING FOR NEW YEAR'S EVE, IRVING?
I THOUGHT I'D JUST SPEND A QUIET EVENING BY MYSELF THIS YEAR.

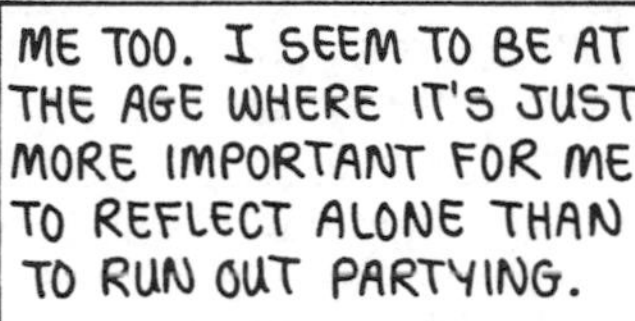
ME TOO. I SEEM TO BE AT THE AGE WHERE IT'S JUST MORE IMPORTANT FOR ME TO REFLECT ALONE THAN TO RUN OUT PARTYING.

YEAH... I KNOW WHAT YOU MEAN...

HI. WHAT ARE YOU TWO DOING FOR NEW YEAR'S EVE?
WE BOTH HAVE DATES WITH OTHER PEOPLE.

TA DA!
I CAN'T GO OUT IN PUBLIC LIKE THIS.

TA DA!
I LOOK RIDICULOUS.

TA DA!
FORGET IT.

CATHY! HOW ARE YOU?!
I'M SIMPLE, DAVID, BUT I'M SECURE.

THE IMPORTANT THING IS TO BE ABLE TO LOOK BACK AT THE PAST YEAR AND SAY, "I HAVE NO REGRETS!"
1982
HAPPY NEW YEAR

I WAS FAIR, THOUGHTFUL, PATIENT, KIND, LOVING, TRUSTWORTHY AND HONEST.

I STUCK TO MY PRINCIPLES, I WORKED TO MY POTENTIAL, AND I BROUGHT JOY TO ALL THOSE AROUND ME !!
BRAVO ! BRAVO !!

I WANTED TO GET ONE LAST LIE IN BEFORE THE CLOCK STRUCK TWELVE.
HAPPY NEW YEAR

AREN'T THOSE NEW BOOTS LOVELY ?

THIS IS A BRAND NEW HEIGHT, A BRAND NEW HEEL, A BRAND NEW STYLE, A BRAND NEW COLOR...
BOOT

OF COURSE, LIKE ANY FINE BOOT, THESE WILL BE TOTALLY RUINED IF YOU EVER WEAR THEM OUT IN THE SNOW.

I'M GLAD TO SEE YOU HUNG ON TO THE ONE IMPORTANT FEATURE.
BOOT

I'M GOING TO READ THE MAGAZINES I BUY... GO TO THE SEMINARS I SIGN UP FOR... TAKE CARE OF WHAT I OWN, VOICE MY OPINIONS, BROADEN MY HORIZONS, MAKE A FORTUNE AND DISCOVER TRUE LOVE !!

THIS IS THE FIRST MONDAY OF A BRAND NEW YEAR, ANDREA ! IT'S ALL WITHIN MY GRASP !! THE WORLD BELONGS TO...

CATHY ?... WHAT HAPPENED ?

MY COFFEE JUST WORE OFF.
365

PRODUCT TESTING, INC. WHAT DO YOU WANT?
GET ME THE DRAPE UPDATE, CHARLENE!
RECEPTIONIST

GET IT YOURSELF!
SOMEONE TOOK THE ARTEX FILE OFF MY DESK!
RECEPTIONIST

TOUGH LUCK!
NO I AM NOT AVAILABLE FOR A MEETING!
RECEPTIONIST

I LOVE IT WHEN THE WHOLE OFFICE IS ON A DIET.
CATHY

YOU'LL NEVER LOSE WEIGHT IF YOU DON'T SET REALISTIC GOALS, CATHY.
I KNOW, ANDREA, AND I HAVE.

IN CALENDAR YEAR 1982, MY GOAL IS TO LOSE THREE POUNDS!!

THREE POUNDS IN A WHOLE YEAR?? THAT ISN'T REALISTIC.
YOU'RE RIGHT.

IT'S TWICE AS MUCH AS I WOUND UP LOSING LAST YEAR.
FLOUR

OOPS! SILLY ME! I WROTE "1981" INSTEAD OF "1982".
OOPS! HA, HA! ME TOO!
WHAT'S WRONG WITH THESE PEOPLE?

EVERY YEAR I HEAR THE SAME CONVERSATION 400 TIMES. "OOPS! OOPS! OOPS!"

IT'S INCREDIBLE THAT PEOPLE CAN'T REMEMBER SUCH A BASIC THING!

RIP!
RIP! RIP

DO YOU KNOW WHY I NEVER LOSE WEIGHT, MOM? IT'S BECAUSE OF THAT DISAPPROVING LOOK YOU GET ON YOUR FACE.
COOKIES

THERE'S NOTHING WRONG WITH ME EATING **ONE** COOKIE... BUT WHEN YOU GIVE ME THAT LOOK, I GET NERVOUS AND DEFENSIVE AND THEN I WANT TO EAT THE WHOLE BOX!
COOKIES

FINE. WHY DON'T I JUST LEAVE THE ROOM?
COOKIES

I CAN FEEL YOUR DISAPPROVING LOOK THROUGH THE WALL!!
COOKIES
Guisewite

OF COURSE YOU DON'T HAVE TO WATCH OVER ME, ANDREA, I'M IN CONTROL OF MY DIET THIS TIME!

I'VE SET REALISTIC GOALS, AND I'M WORKING TOWARDS THEM SLOWLY AND SENSIBLY!
I'M PROUD OF YOU, CATHY. KEEP UP THE GOOD WORK!

SLAM!

PEOPLE WHO HAVE A CHEESECAKE IN THE REFRIGERATOR WILL SAY ANYTHING.
Guisewite

I LOVE GOING GROCERY SHOPPING WHEN I'M STILL DRESSED IN MY OFFICE CLOTHES.

I FEEL SO PROFESSIONAL... ...SO EFFICIENT...

I CAN'T GET THESE STUPID PLASTIC BAGS OPEN!!

...SO DYNAMIC... SO RESPECTABLE...
Guisewite

I'M GOING TO THROW THE REST OF THE COOKIES DOWN THE GARBAGE DISPOSAL AND NEVER EAT ANOTHER FATTENING THING!

EAT
EAT
EAT
EAT

I'M GOING TO THROW THE REST OF THE ICE CREAM DOWN THE GARBAGE DISPOSAL AND NEVER EAT ANOTHER FATTENING THING!!

THIS CEREMONY IS STARTING TO LOSE ITS MEANING.
donuts

EXCITING NEWS, CATHY. I'VE HIRED AN ASSISTANT FOR YOU.
OH, MR. PINKLEY, THIS IS WONDERFUL!
PINKLEY

I'VE ALWAYS DREAMED OF HAVING A BRIGHT YOUNG WOMAN BY MY SIDE TO TRAIN.
PINKLEY

SHE WILL BECOME MY CONFIDANTE! I WILL BE HER MENTOR! TOGETHER, WE'LL...
THIS IS ZEKE. HE STARTS TODAY.

ZEKE?...UH, HOW DO YOU DO ...
MY DESK IS TOO SMALL. THE COFFEE'S TERRIBLE. AND I WANTED AN OFFICE WITH A WINDOW.

IF PINKLEY EXPECTS ME TO DO THIS GARBAGE FOR A MEASLY $23,000 A YEAR, HE CAN FORGET IT!

$23,000 A YEAR? MY ASSISTANT IS MAKING $23,000 A YEAR??!

MR. PINKLEY, ISN'T THERE SOMETHING YOU'D LIKE TO SAY ABOUT THIS??

YOU PROMISED NOT TO TELL!!

I KNOW I SHOULD GIVE MR. PINKLEY A BIG LECTURE ...BUT LET'S FACE IT, ANDREA, CRYING WORKS. IT'S A DECISION WE ALL HAVE TO MAKE.
PRODUCT TESTING INC.

DO WE CONFRONT SITUATIONS WITH INTELLIGENCE AND DIGNITY, OR DO WE RESORT TO THE CHEAP--BUT EFFECTIVE--TACTIC OF TEARS?
PRODUCT TESTING INC.

MR. PINKLEY, I... WAAAAH!!

MY INSTINCTS TOOK OVER.
PRODUCT TESTING INC.

ON JANUARY 1, MY GOAL WAS TO LOSE 15 POUNDS AND GET EVERY ASPECT OF MY LIFE ORGANIZED TO PERFECTION.

ON JANUARY 7, MY GOAL WAS TO HAVE A SEMBLANCE OF ORDER AND PERIODIC SELF-DISCIPLINE.

TODAY, 16 DAYS INTO THE NEW YEAR, I'M CLINGING TO THE SHREDS OF 23-SELF-IMPROVEMENT PROJECTS AND MY ONLY GOAL IS TO NOT WAKE UP WITH A HEADACHE.

YOU'RE AMAZING, CATHY.
I KNOW. THIS IS THE BEST I'VE EVER DONE.

WOMEN WERE CONDITIONED FOR TWO RESPONSES, MR. PINKLEY. WE SMILE OR WE CRY.

EVEN WHEN WE'RE FURIOUS, WE EXPRESS IT BY CRYING OR SMILING.

I JUST WANT YOU TO KNOW THAT UNDER THIS CHEERY SMILE IS THE HEART OF A WOMAN WHO WANTS TO RIP YOUR FACE OFF FOR PAYING MY ASSISTANT $23,000 A YEAR.
PINKLEY

WHAT DO YOU MEAN, HE DIDN'T TAKE YOU SERIOUSLY?

MR. PINKLEY IS PAYING MY ASSISTANT $6000 MORE THAN ME, AND I'M NOT GOING TO STAND FOR IT.
BREAD

I WILL NOT TOLERATE THIS KIND OF ABUSE, MR. PINKLEY. EITHER GIVE ME A $7000 RAISE, OR I AM WALKING AWAY FROM THIS JOB AND NEVER COMING BACK!!
BREAD

GOOD MORNING, CHARLENE. TELL PINKLEY I WANT TO SEE HIM!
HE'S NOT COMING IN TODAY.
RECEPTIONIST

THERE'S NOTHING WORSE THAN GOING THROUGH THE DAY WITH AN 11,000-CALORIE SPEECH IN YOUR STOMACH.
CATHY
Guisewite

YOOHOO, CATHY! I PICKED YOU UP SOME FRUIT AND SHELF ORGANIZERS AND I HAD A THOUGHT ABOUT IRVING... ...NOW, DON'T YOU THINK YOU...

WHAT ARE YOU DOING HERE, DEAR??

CATHY'S BEEN HAVING A PROBLEM WITH HER BOSS AND I THOUGHT I COULD HELP OUT.

WELL! ISN'T THAT JUST LIKE A FATHER TO TRY TO PRY INTO HIS DAUGHTER'S BUSINESS!
Guisewite

NO, IRVING. I MOST CERTAINLY DO NOT WANT TO GO OUT TONIGHT.

I'VE BEEN RUNNING SINCE 6:30 THIS MORNING, AND THE LAST THING ON EARTH I WANT TO DO IS TO TRY TO BE CUTE AND COHERENT FOR ANOTHER FIVE HOURS!!

I MISS YOU, TOO, MY DARLING!!

THE NEW ROMANCE.
Guisewite

LET ME SEE IF I HAVE THIS RIGHT, DEAR. I BUTT INTO CATHY'S LIFE IN THE AREA OF NUTRITION. YOU BUTT INTO HER LIFE IN THE AREA OF BUSINESS.

I BUTT IN FOR GROOMING AND DATING. YOU BUTT IN FOR HOME SECURITY AND INVESTMENTS.

OH, WE'RE SUCH A MODERN COUPLE!

WE'RE SHARING OUR WORKLOAD!
Guisewite

THE SAME THING HAPPENED TO ME, CATHY, SO I QUIT AND MADE THEM HIRE ME BACK FOR $7,000 MORE A YEAR!

HA, HA! I GOT AN $8,000 RAISE AND A COMPANY CAR!

HA, HA! I GOT A $9,000 RAISE, A COMPANY CAR, AND 500 SHARES OF STOCK!!

HE WHO LIES LAST GETS STUCK WITH THE CHECK.
Guisewite

THIS MAGAZINE TAUGHT ME HOW TO NEGOTIATE A TWO MILLION DOLLAR CONTRACT.
SAVVY

THIS ONE TAUGHT ME HOW TO ANALYZE ECONOMIC INDICATORS AND RESTRUCTURE DATA FEEDBACK PROGRAMS FOR MAXIMUM CAPITAL GAIN.
SAVVY

HOW EXCITING! WHAT DID YOU DO AT THE OFFICE TODAY??

WE SPENT THE WHOLE DAY FIGHTING OVER WHO STOLE CHARLENE'S BOYSENBERRY YOGURT OUT OF THE OFFICE REFRIGERATOR.
Guisewite

YES, WE HAVE MANY NICE DESK CALENDARS LEFT. YOU WANT THE PREP OR THE ANTI-PREP ?
CALENDARS

THE CAT OR THE ANTI-CAT ?

THE PIG OR THE ANTI-PIG ?

WHATEVER HAPPENED TO THE GOOD OLD DAYS WHEN I COULD BUY SOMETHING WITHOUT TAKING SIDES ?
Guisewite

I HAD A WONDERFUL TIME WITH YOU TONIGHT, CATHY.
I HAD A WONDERFUL TIME TOO, IRVING.

MAYBE...UH..MAYBE YOU'D LIKE TO SLIP INTO SOMETHING MORE COMFORTABLE.
OOH..I'D LOVE TO GET INTO SOMETHING MORE COMFORTABLE..

WHEW! THIS FEELS MUCH BETTER!

YOU SUGGESTED IT!!!
Guisewite

IF I KISS THIS MAN GOODNIGHT, I WILL ENCOURAGE HIM AND I'M NOT SURE I WANT TO DO THAT.

THEN AGAIN, IF I DON'T KISS HIM, IT WILL BE DEVASTATING TO HIS EGO AND WILL PROBABLY RUIN HIS WHOLE WEEK.

I'D BETTER KISS HIM. JUST ONE, LITTLE, TEENSY KISS...
OKAY WITH YOU IF I JUST SPEND THE NIGHT ?

WHY AM I ALWAYS HAVING THE WRONG CONVERSATION ?
Guisewite

WHY DON'T I EVER KNOW WHAT'S GOING ON IN MY RELATIONSHIPS, ANDREA?
YOU DON'T KNOW WHAT'S GOING ON?

NO. I NEVER KNOW WHAT'S GOING ON. EVEN WHEN I'M STANDING RIGHT THERE LOOKING AT IT, I NEVER SEE WHAT ANYTHING IS SUPPOSED TO MEAN.

LOVE IS LIKE THE SATELLITE WEATHER MAP.
Guisewite

ARE YOU DEPRESSED BECAUSE IT'S YOUR BIRTHDAY TODAY, MOM?
OH, DON'T BE SILLY, CATHY.
CATHY

WHEN YOU GET TO MY AGE, BIRTHDAYS ARE JUST ANOTHER DAY! HA, HA, HA!
CATHY

I DO THIS EVERY DAY.
Guisewite

I'M $80 IN THE HOLE, AND I HAVE 80 PROJECTS OVERDUE AT WORK.

IT'S BEEN 80 DAYS SINCE I HAD A DECENT DATE, 80 HOURS SINCE I WASHED THE DISHES, AND 80 WEEKS SINCE I REALLY COMMUNICATED WITH MY MOTHER.

TO CONSOLE MYSELF, I'M GOING TO GO SIT ON MY 80-YEAR-OLD CARPETING AND EAT 80 M&M'S.

I AM AN 80's WOMAN.
Guisewite